Love So Pure
IN THE EYE OF TIME

GESIERE BRISIBE-DORGU

Copyright © 2020 by Gesiere Brisibe-Dorgu.

ISBN: Softcover   978-1-950596-65-2

All rights reserved. No part of this publication may be reproduced, stored in a retrieval system or transmitted in any way by any means, electronic, mechanical, photocopy, recording or otherwise without the prior permission of the author except as provided by USA copyright law.

This novel is a work of fiction. Names, descriptions, entities, and incidents included in the story are products of the author's imagination. Any resemblance to actual persons, events, and entities is entirely coincidental.

Printed in the United States of America.

To order additional copies of this book, contact:
Bookwhip
1-855-339-3589
www.bookwhip.com

DEDICATION

To my beloved transited parents, Chief Festus Pouke Brisibe and Mrs. Poun-ere Brisibe who sowed in me, the seed of right thinking and right doing.

ACKNOWLEDGMENTS

Several persons contributed in no small way to the successful completion of this book.

My special thanks go to the following who contributed in different ways to this success story: Ezeako Odi, who carefully perused the original manuscript over a period of several days. Jones Ike, who also proof read the manuscript and encouraged me a great deal.

The late Sam Aideyan, a bright and intelligent young man whose critique and suggestions were very helpful. My assistants and secretaries especially, James Welson for typing the original manuscript.

Finally, a resounding thanks to my dedicated and tireless 'Volunteer Corp' members; Capt. James Femowei (Rtd), Emenekeowei Amaduobogha (Amadu) and late Francis Ezonbode Femowei. Without your help, the follow-up and running around would have been quite difficult. I am very grateful - Ado-o!

FOREWORD

This book will take you through times, spheres and back. So engaging, one gets lost in it easily. Not many people understand, appreciate or comprehend the import, content and components of the concept of reincarnation. In fact, the subject is rarely discussed in the present Pentecostal euphoria. This is not surprising because much of the theory of spiritual rebirth is shrouded in myth and mythology. This apart, the manifestation of these components vary from continent to continent and peoples to peoples. No one practice is the same anywhere.

That being said, it is pertinent to note that there are some cases that researchers have found to be genuine. The following cases were reported by the 'Reincarnation after Death?' website. A girl named Purnima Ekanayake from Sri Lanka, was exhaustively studied by psychology professor Erlendur Haraldsson who confirmed her story to be true. A boy, Cameron Macaulay from Scotland was investigated by psychologist Jim Tucker, who found his reincarnation story to be true. Two Indian professionals, Professor Atreva and Dr. Jumana Prasad investigated the case of an Indian boy named Munna and found him to be an authentic reincarnated being.

The fascinating similarities between John F. Kennedy and Lincoln have been touted for years as proof of the possibility that the two were or are actually one and the same person, albeit appearing at different time periods. There are many religious theories in contemporary society that appear to be in sharp contrast with ancient belief systems that allow for a soul to manifest in another body after a period of rest in what might be termed the spirit world. Some would refer to this situation as Life after life, a true indication that life is actually without end.

Love So Pure is a passionate recount of man's essence in life as linked to the divine purpose of our creation in its complete and true form. The book captures a vivid theorization that the human soul lives again in a new body after someone's physical death. The author has successfully animated the reader to subconsciously embark on a spiritual voyage of self-discovery. It is finesse in prose to be able to create a nexus between hazy traditional beliefs and practices and contemporary religious practices.

Love So Pure is a driving force for animate beings who want to seek the hidden doors to the realities of creation. It also serves as preparatory recipe for one to meet his/her ultimate Creator through embracing the finest virtues of life such as tolerance, empathy, patience, peace and unconditional love. To the sober seeker, the ideas contained therein are soothing tonics for the Soul. The simplicity in language and choice of locality (the Niger Delta area of Nigeria) has exposed the author's naturalist bent in re-awakening necessary traditional values without compromising higher spiritual values. This cannot be overemphasized in the present day where the young ones hardly show courtesy when responding to older persons. The Western concept of handshake and a bold 'hello' or 'hi' to parents and elders has since overturned cherished customary modes of salutation in many parts of Africa. The reader will however find humor in pronouncing some Ijaw(Izon) names, terminologies, practices and thought processes. The Ijaw or Izon nationality is believed to the fourth largest ethnic group in Nigeria.

The style of Prose in Love So Pure reveals the true nature and character of the author as a skilled writer. This book is a rich source and inspiration for those who seek cosmic wisdom. It is a study guide for metaphysics and all who seek the truth in transmigration and metempsychosis.

Here we find an individual's personal commitment to the world, preaching the gospel of divine favor and Love and identifying the meaning and purpose of Life. It is a fitting path to activate a true rebirth of the soul in relation to the law of Cause and Effect: that what one does in this present life has serious consequences in the here and now, as well as the spiritual realm.

Finally, the book raises pertinent questions and points to ponder as to the real identity and divine mission of the author. In the words of a one-time cabinet Minister of the Federal Republic of Nigeria Dr. M T Akobo: who are you Gesi? What are you Lady D? What is your goal in this life? Are you a teacher … preacher, prophet or what? On my part, I think and strongly believe that she is simply an embodiment of the virtues of life, a lover of culture and a Lady with a heart of Love So Pure!

Bakumor Smith Yolo

CHAPTER 1

I am tempted to say, fate must have arranged things because I was not really interested in leaving the cozy comfort of my bed. It was a Saturday and I was at the Eselemo Civic Centre for a function organized for one of the political bigwigs of the ruling party. My friend Kene-ama who was a member of the organizing committee had persuaded, indeed pressured me to attend.

"What will you be doing at home on a Saturday all by your own lonely self?" He had asked, a day before the event. Being aware that I had just quit my job as the manager of a private telecommunications company because of differences in opinion with the director, who was becoming increasingly overbearing anyway, he wanted me to shake off the moodiness I was feeling.

"Besides, you don't know who you may meet there. A lot of important persons will attend and you may just make an acquaintance that could turn out to be useful later." He said, smiling broadly.

I considered the situation, weighed my options which were not many and since I really had nothing doing, I agreed to go. "You won't regret this decision, O'l boy," Kene-ama assured. "There will be a lot to eat and drink. Who knows, you may even find a charming companion!" He said, winking mischievously.

My friend was aware that I had been estranged from my wife for some time and I guessed from the sly grin on his face that he was Gesiere Brisibe-Dorgu 16 hoping to 'hook' me up with some 'nice' lady. The marriage had hit the waves hard after less than five years. We had grown apart so quickly and I could not comprehend why or how. The whole thing kind of crept up on me I guess. We just could not arrive at a consensus on anything, from deciding the number of children we should have to the investments that were viable and whose friends were more important and other seemingly 'trivial' issues. There was no need to seek the services of a prophet or psychic to tell us that our union was a hopeless mismatch. This incompatibility virtually accompanied us wherever we went and no one was in doubt that we were on our way to saying, 'to your tent O spouse!'

As the party got underway, true to my friend's words, the civic center overflowed with dignitaries from within and outside the State. I sat somewhere in middle of the hall and watched the proceedings with little interest. It was more like a political party convention really, as important and not so important individuals jostled for attention. Kene-ama was doing a great job scurrying from place to place in a spirited effort to ensure that everything went well. Several people had delivered speeches and the whole event was becoming increasingly boring to me. I looked at my wristwatch and seriously considered leaving. I could always see Kene-ama later and apologize for leaving without telling him I reasoned, as my attention momentarily turned to other guests seated nearby.

While doing so, I dabbled in mental mathematics , calculating the number of ladies in proportion to the men. The ladies were so many and all were gorgeously dressed, mostly in a variety of colorful and expensive looking traditional attires.

Trust Nigerian ladies and fashion, I sighed. Some were with partners while others appeared to be alone. In spite of their good looks though, none caught my fancy. This was understandable since my interest in the opposite sex was at almost zero level. Keneama had tried to introduce me to some charming ones in the past without success. As far as I was concerned, what I had experienced with my wife was too painful for me to consider dating anytime soon.

I had just decided that there was nothing to be gained from remaining at the function and was about to leave, when I saw HER!

She was sitting on the third row from the front and I wondered why I had not noticed her earlier. I sat back and observed her closely.

The more I looked at her, the more like iron filings to magnet she attracted me. It was not as if she was particularly outstanding in her mode of dressing. It was the way she carried herself, her mien and poise. Call it charisma if you like and yes, she was also very beautiful. Still determined to leave, I thought it fortunate that I had to pass close to her on my way out. As I stood up and walked towards where she sat, jumping over a few empty chairs, people stared at me curiously but I didn't care.

I suddenly felt so light-headed and gay that I was surprised at myself! "Hello, my soul!" I said when I finally got to her side. A few young men standing nearby overheard what I said and shook their heads, smiling knowingly. As I took a closer look at her, I knew with a certainty that was uncanny that she was the rarest of all finds, a true soul twin, the missing half of my being! She looked piercingly into my eyes and smiled.

"Where have you been hiding, dear one?"

Come, come away from this suffocating place, she seemed to be saying after this question, as she continued to look at me quizzically. I stretched out my right hand and she took it wordlessly and led the way out of the hall into the bright sunshine outside.

"That is my car." I said, pointing to a modest looking red Ford Cortina. The parking lot was jam-packed but I had managed to squeeze the Cortina into a corner.

"Let's go somewhere for a drink." I offered.

"By all means, we have a lifetime of catching up to do." She responded as we introduced ourselves and got into the car. Her name was Zibo-ere and mine of course was Layefa. As we drove out of the parking lot, my mind was in turmoil. What was happening to me? Was I in a trance? But that could not be, since I was conscious and conversing with this strange but already familiar person! I was getting dizzy from the commotion of emotions welling up in my heart and head. As if reading my mind Zibo-ere called my name softly.

"Layefa, is it not absolutely mind-boggling for us to have come together in this manner? It is as if one has been transported into another world. To all intents and purposes you are a stranger to me yet, I feel certain that I know you intimately. Rather confusing and paradoxical I dare say, but it is a fact!"

I agreed and told her I felt the same way. Our encounter was the strangest thing that had happened to me. I already felt that she would play a key role in my life. This may sound crazy and incredible because we had just met but truth be told, that was how I felt. Then seemingly out of the blues, memories of our past relationship seeped into my consciousness. I turned to her and was about to say something when she grabbed my left hand.

"Do you remember the vow we made to each other at the river bank that beautiful moon lit night? The entire village was asleep. Not a flicker of light was seen anywhere. Great grandmother Tarenemi had just finished telling one of her captivating stories by firelight. As everyone present, children and adults alike sleepily got off to bed, someone whispered a devastating new into my ears. The fellow said you were critically ill, in fact, at the point of death! Sleep immediately sped out of my sight and I ran like a gold medal Olympian over to your house. I breathlessly rushed over to where you were lying down and gingerly removed the cloth that covered your face and what did I see? Your white teeth exposed in a silent mischievous laugh! I was really angry at you for frightening me so badly and my first instinct was to give you a dirty slap but I refrained from doing so because you hugged me so tightly. I could not hold back the tears as you scooped me into your arms and rocked me like a baby, singing soulful melodies of love and begging to be forgiven. When at last I said I had forgiven you, we strolled arm-in-arm to the river bank, sat on a felled palm tree and talked until the early hours of the morning."

I nodded as I began to recollect bits and pieces of that incident. It was as if someone had pushed me into a room full of old pictures and turned on a bright light.

"But my dear Zibo-ere, that must be countless ages ago!" I exclaimed.

"How could you have remembered what happened to us so vividly? To have totally recalled where we were and what we did then is incredible, unbelievable!"

I paused for a while, trying to piece events together. In those days, each village or hamlet was a 'State' of its own. People did whatever they deemed fit. Survival of the fittest was the norm. If a neighboring village offended yours, you could, under cover of night sack the entire village. In fact, weak villages were expected to share whatever wealth they had equally with their stronger neighbors as a sort of insurance to guarantee their continued survival.

"Ah, Layefa, you are also beginning to recall how life was back then!" Zibo-ere remarked.

"Do not be surprised, Looking at you brings back memories of long forgotten occurrences," I told her.

"In fact Zibo-ere," I continued, looking sideways at her.

"History has it that a name-sake of mine, who lived in Ebiama some two hundred or so years ago, was one of the greatest warriors in the Niger Delta. The elders unanimously named him Ama-Olotu after he single-handedly sacked Eyesin, a village of about fifty families. This feat was achieved with just a bag full of potent diri and raw physical strength. The story goes that it was an unforgettable day in Ebiama. Every maiden in the village wanted to be Layefa's wife and every young man wanted to be like him. A proclamation was made that all storytellers for generations to come must tell the story of the great Layefa, the hero of Ebiama."

As I recalled this incident in the history of Ebiama, it occurred to me that I might have been a key player. Amazingly, the day of the great victory feast now came into focus in my mind's eye! Ten sister villages as well as the entire Bolou-Toru and Kala-Toru clans were invited. The war canoes brought by the villages and clans were a sight to behold, as they paddled to the shore.

Bolou-Toru clan came in a big flaming blood-red canoe. Their long paddles were painted red, yellow, white and black. Palm fronds tacked to the seats of the canoe were half immersed in water. The warriors, twelve in number, were attired in deep blue and white singlets. They sang the hero's song in unison with the swish of the paddles sweeping through the water. Opu-Toru's canoe was less colorful. It had only yellow and blue stripes on the sides and their paddles were dotted with green and red paint.

Their warriors, also twelve, had their faces painted menacingly with blue lines drawn across the bridges of their noses and foreheads. They danced and jumped in the most fast-paced Ogele ever seen. The twelve warriors from Kala-Toru also came in a blood-red canoe with blue and red colored paddles and palm fronds at the sides of the canoe and trailing several yards behind in the water. Their bodies were painted red and they chanted war songs so loudly and piercingly that some said the coconut trees lining the efinkiriyo swayed in rhythm with them!

"Aha!" Zibo-ere exclaimed, also remembering the event.

"As all the warriors jumped down from their canoes along the shore, Layefa, wearing the multicolored regalia of a hero was there to receive them. The Kala-Toru warriors carried him shoulder high in a fierce Ogele around the village and the reverberations shook the earth! My aunt Ebiteme told us about the numerous unseen dancers, a lot more than the villagers and visitors put together, that participated at the feast. She said both sides of the river were fully packed with beings rejoicing with us and the sight took her breath away."

Zibo-ere and I appeared to recall this historical occasion at Ebiama so clearly that it dawned on us that we were having a peculiar experience. I wondered whether it was some kind of divine manipulation or an alien intervention. What else could I attribute it to other than the supernatural? After all, we were both just ordinary, regular human beings living ordinary lives. I was known to be a focused man with a sense of direction far removed from religious zealousness or deep meditation, which some people believe elicits extra-sensory perception. With this background, it was difficult to imagine that we were being specially favored with this glimpse into the far past. What some would term time travel backwards.

This was the only way I could logically or illogically explain what we were experiencing. How else could someone like me who even finds it difficult to recall simple historical facts of a few decades suddenly remember these events in my extremely distant past life so clearly?

It's to say the least, unfathomable. Universal mind and Almighty Creator of everything, make me understand what is happening to me, I prayed silently. Grant me the wisdom to discern the meaning of this sudden recollection, the purpose of it and what it portends. Zibo-ere, who was equally perplexed, was also apparently praying.

"Layefa, my dear." She said suddenly. "I pray that the Almighty will reveal the true purpose of this strange experience we are having."

As if in answer to our supplications, scenes from my remote past life now came in a flood. Years ago, I read something about people being able to remember past events through hypnotism and wondered whether I was being remotely hypnotized and if so, by whom? But what about Zibo-ere?

'It's definitely too much of a stretch to think or imagine an invisible hypnotist manipulating your lives O'l boy!' I cautioned myself. Hypnotherapy was and still is done in a controlled environment. The hypnotist gradually regresses the person to the desired age or period to enable full or partial recall. There is controversy of course, about how reliable such a method is especially among those who do not believe in reincarnation. This set of people assert that once you die, you are gone, finished! You transit never to come back to planet earth!

However, many others including traditional Africans, believe firmly in reincarnation. It was a common practice among some Izon people of the Niger Delta to make lacerations on the body of a dead child thought to have been born several times, each time dying in infancy. With these markings before burial, the offending child was bound to be recognized if it appeared again.

There was a particularly interesting case in Eyesin worth mentioning. Beni-ere's chocolate-complexioned baby boy was born with horrendous scars all over his frail body. The belief was that it was the same baby she gave birth to a few years back who died in infancy. Beni-ere had lost three babies previously and on the last occasion, she decided to give the dead child 'farewell' marks all over its little body before burying him. Even skeptics were therefore convinced beyond reasonable doubt, when this scared baby survived and grew up to become a fearless warrior.

He was called Ebamua, meaning you are not going back. Zibo-ere also remembered Beni-ere's case. The baby was so fearsome looking at birth that the poor woman could not stand its sight. It took the gentle counseling of the Orukare-ere, who prophesied that the child would grow up to be a blessing to the whole village, for her to go back home and nurse it.

Anyway, back to the present! Still perplexed about our inexplicable recollections, we sat down to a hearty meal of Osun and Banga soup. I watched Zibo-ere surreptitiously as we ate, wondering if she was not some wise spirit planted on me by Krekre, the famous wicked wizard in my village! A very good friend of mine Keme-owei, never failed to mention the wizard's exploits in the village whenever we met and I always laughed at him, telling him to go read his Bible or some other spiritual book. He would warn me about how some followers of the Bible had been particularly singled out and tormented, not only by the wizard but also by the witch, diriguo-ere.

"Let's face it, Layefa," my friend would say, "This is the twentieth century and I agree that Christianity has been with us for quite some time now but can we run away from ourselves? There are so many things about the world we cannot fathom. I think it is dangerous to go ridiculing things you do not understand. You only end up confusing gullible people and even yourself because you lack in-depth knowledge of your beliefs to back up your claims. Try to study and understand our traditional systems and beliefs before you discard them for foreign ones. A word is enough for the…… I will counsel you again my friend, when the need arises." His usual parting shot would be, "remote control emi-o!"

I sighed and smiled slightly as I recalled this conversation and Zibo-ere immediately reached for my hands.

"Do not be troubled my dear, all is well!" She said this with such soul-stirring smile that I could not resist but reciprocate with an equally warm smile. "I am sure you are right, Zibo-ere.

I am sure you're right!" We sat silently for a while, each deep in thought until a light touch from her hand brought me back to the present.

"Did you notice the type of fish the steward served us?" She asked.

"Yes, of course! The almighty 'iced fish' without which many families would not be able to eat fish at all."

"Layefa, what has the world come to?" She lamented.

Of course, she was remembering the old times when nets were not needed to catch fish for meals. All one had to do was paddle about one nautical mile or less offshore and so much fish would have jumped into the canoe! It was always fun to throw some back into the river because there was no need to hoard. If one needed bigger fish, canoes with leftover food would be submerged in a few feet of water before retiring for the night. A haul of fish and lobsters of all sizes was guaranteed the next morning. Sometimes, one would just stand at the shallow end of the river and catch all the fish and crawfish needed for a hearty meal, with bare hands! All that is of course history. It is now imported frozen fish that is generally eaten. Hmmmm!

The world had changed so much over time and as I tried to place the time frame of our former existence or existences, I could not help but speculate about the relationship Zibo-ere and I had. Were we married or just good friends? It was not clear in my mind and I was reluctant to ask her, though I felt certain she knew. She might have assumed that I also knew. I honestly was not sure and was seriously tempted to ask but I dare not. Call it cowardice or foolishness if you will. My goodness, what is this? Am I struggling with my ego or what! I sighed inwardly.

CHAPTER 2

While still battling with these confusing thoughts, it occurred to me to find out if she was married. A sudden devastating fear gripped me. What if she was married with or even without children but still, married? Hey, get a grip on yourself, I silently admonished. Why should it matter if this beloved 'stranger' was married or not?

You are all mixed up like an infatuated teenager. If not adequately checked, some screws could jolly well come loose in your brain my man, my rational mind cautioned. Properly translated, that would mean STARK RAVING MAD! So take several deep breaths and relax and let things flow in divine order. After this self-admonition, I calmed down.

Having finished our meal, Zibo-ere suggested we leave. She stood up and I followed suit after paying for the food. We walked outside to my car and as I got in, I noticed that she looked tense.

I also noticed for the first time how much her skin glittered. I was impressed that it had not been spoilt by the toxic creams commonly used by many women. Her face looked sculptured, with huge brown deep-set eyes and full ebony black lips. She was at least five feet seven inches tall and walked with the gait of a gazelle.

Temearau-O! I exclaimed mutely. I suddenly realized with unshakeable certainty that I would never be able to let this woman out of my sight again. Oh ancestors, I begged. Please tell me what's happening to me! Have I been irrevocably bewitched? Why am I so gloriously happy? Happy? Yes, happy and confused or hallucinating or whatever, I really didn't care!

"Now Layefa, have we come full cycle?" She asked suddenly, startling me out of my reverie.

"Ehn, what did you say?"

"Is it possible that we have made the rounds and have come full cycle?" She repeated, a dreamy almost trancelike look on her face. I squirmed uneasily in my seat. She continued.

"You know, when my aunt Ebiteme told a gathering of all diriolotu, the men and women who claimed to be the greatest soothsayers, prophets and seers in all of the Niger Delta that many of them were sent by Temearau from other worlds to help build up Izon-otu, they laughed at her. She called them fellow travelers and told them that, know it or not, they were centuries old. Some of them charged at her in anger and shaking her vigorously, threatened to beat her up. They even called her an evil dirigwo-ere.

She just smiled tolerantly and called them fools and fake seers and prophets. They were sternly warned to reflect deeply on what she had said and commune more fervently with the all-knowing and invisible 'big mind' for a clear insight into their true mission on earth." As if on a remote-controlled movie screen, I mentally conjured a picture of my uncle and the anda-olotuowei, marching towards our house. Seething with anger, they complained to my father about Ebiteme's audacious utterances.

"Zibo-ere, I remember the incident quite well. I even recall my uncle's words about your aunt's boldness as he complained to my father. But my dear, what has that incident got to do with us? You asked if we have come full cycle. Exactly what do you mean?" She gently took my right hand in hers and looked searchingly at me. Trying to discern something perhaps? I wondered. Maybe a confirmation of what she already knew?

"Before I answer your question, let's go home" She said. Seeing the surprised and a bit panicky look on my face, she smiled and then laughed out loud.

"What are you afraid of, Layefa? You do have a home, don't you?

Do not be afraid. Home is either my place or yours. My husband and child will understand that you are my missing link when they see us together. I also feel certain that your wife and children will not feel threatened when they see us together. This is because we are special, you and I. We are super beings!"

There it is I thought, not too happily. So she is married and even has a child!

"Oh!" I responded weakly.

"I am not married….anymore. My wife and I separated due to irreconcilable differences. We can go to my two-bedroom flat, if you like. I hope you were joking when you said we are super beings? I mean, I know something extraordinary has happened to us, is indeed happening to us but I won't go so far as to say we are super beings! Look at me! I am quite ordinary. Born to normal parents. My father was a court clerk, now a trader and my mother, a farmer and fisher-woman."

"Oh, keep quiet Layefa!" she said.

"No more questions until we get home. By the way, we will go to my place first. Thereafter, if still necessary, we shall go to your flat."

As we drove through the congested streets of Eselemo, everything and everyone looked absolutely normal. Taxi drivers honked their horns ceaselessly and hurled abuses at motorcyclists and motorists. Pedestrians struggled with motorcycles and cars for right-of-way as usual and cursed and swore at each other.

"Hey, make you look me-oh! Yeye man!"

"Look mister, if you kill me, you go see pepper-o!"

"Oga driver, you no fit drive? Abeg, comot for road make I pass!"

"Foolish man! Remove your scrap for road-boh!"

These were regular features of a busy street on a normal working day. I wondered why everything looked so normal when my world had literally been turned upside-down. Driving carefully and following Zibo-ere's directions did not prevent my wanting to shout at the top of my voice.

Hey! look here you people out there! Don't look so normal! Something momentous and incomprehensible has just happened and is still happening to me! Do you know that I, Layefa, could have been traversing the earth for a thousand years? Yes, I may even be from another planet with a special mission here on earth, which will be revealed to me by this wondrous woman sitting beside me. Listen to me, world! Pay attention and marvel, you hear me! Everyone do you hear me?

I of course suppressed this urge and drove on, making faces at passers-by. Some responded by cursing, their outspread fingers inches from my face.

"Waaka! Stupid man!"

Presently, Ziboere pointed to a fenced compound with a red gate. It was an imposing bungalow surrounded by several varieties of tropical flowers and fruit trees.

"That is my house. Just hunk the horn and someone will open the gate."

I did and the gate was opened by a stout mean-looking man wearing loose trousers and a red T-shirt. He must have been between twenty five to thirty years old and about five feet seven inches tall. We drove in and parked in the drive way. I must confess here and now friends. I was surprised to see a six-foot, red haired, barefooted white man wearing a pair of brown shorts and grey shirt come out of the house to greet us, well, to put it more accurately, Zibo-ere. I noticed his light brown eyes because of the twinkle in them. I was slightly apprehensive and a little uneasy since I did not expect her to be married to a white man. I admit that I did not ask her to give me details of her family when she first dropped the 'unpleasant' surprise.

All the same, seeing him did not help matters. I figured that our present situation was weird enough and further inquiries about a foreign spouse would only compound issues, so I kept my surprise to myself.

Oh Temearau! What a position to be in. The whole thing seemed unreal to me. In any case, I braced myself for the worst.

"Hello honey!" The husband beamed, embracing his wife lovingly. He turned to me and shook my hand warmly.

"Welcome! Please come right in!"

Following them into their tastefully furnished and spacious living room, it occurred to me that Zibo-ere and I were not and could not be in the same category of self-employed regular people.

How could I compare myself to her when she appeared to be living a life of affluence?

Even before we took our seats, a steward was already waiting.

"What will you have Sir?" He asked courteously.

"Any soft drink will be okay, thank you!" I responded.

"Layefa, please relax and feel at home. Dinner will be ready soon." Zibo-ere said and disappeared into another part of the house. The steward soon came with the drink and set it on a stool beside me.

Her husband meanwhile sat with me in the living room.

"May I welcome you once again to our home! My name is Bilflow. Bilflow Forest."

"I am Layefa. Thanks for your kind reception Mr. Forest."

"Ah, Bilflow is fine. Everyone calls me Bilflow so feel free to call me that as well." He said, smiling.

Bilflow was a man who loved to talk. He talked about diverse things before telling me about how he met Zibo-ere. Why he loved our country and people, particularly the Izons. He recalled how Zibo-ere's family was not too pleased when she introduced him to them as her future husband. The idea of having a pena-owei, white man, as a son-in-law was unacceptable. This had never happened in the village before and they were not sure about the general reaction of the community. In all honesty, only prostitutes were usually linked to white men amorously at that time. But after persistent pressure from him and seeing that he was a humble man and very respectful of their culture, they relented. One thing, though, the family insisted that he must marry their daughter according to the traditions of her people, before the so-called 'white wedding' could be done. Bilflow said he was quite willing and happy to oblige as he considered the Izon culture a rich one.

Presently, dinner was announced and Bilflow invited me to join him at table. He sat at the head of the table and Zibo-ere soon joined us, sitting to the right of her husband. Bilflow continued his narrative through dinner.

"I can see that Bill has been regaling you with tales of our odogboro dein, the traditional marriage ceremony." Zibo-ere said, smiling.

"I don't blame Bill for relating the event at every opportunity. It was a celebration to remember. My mother had insisted that the marriage must be done according to our original tradition. She was not interested in the modernized or abridged version. I want people to know that you are a respectable, responsible and intelligent girl, my child and not a wayward wayside girl even though you are marrying someone from a faraway land." she told me.

CHAPTER 3

After dinner, Zibo-ere and Bilflow excused themselves and left me alone in the living room. I was just settling down to ponder my situation when a little girl of about five years walked in. She looked at me in an uncertain manner. I smiled and beckoned to her. Smiling shyly, she came over to me. A biracial child with the features of a goddess, her luscious reddish brown hair reached down to her waist. She definitely had an angelic appearance.

"Hello my dear. You're a beautiful little angel, you know that?"

"Thank you very much, Sir! I am Ebiere, who are you?" She asked.

"My name is Layefa, pretty one."

"Oh, you must be my mummy's brother or cousin. You look like her." I stared at her in surprise.

"I'm hungry. Come and eat with me." She invited.

"Thank you my dear, I've already eaten."

Bilflow and Zibo-ere came in and overheard the child's invitation. He took her hand and led her gently to the dining table and put her comfortably on her chair then came over to join us, sitting close to Zibo-ere. There was a brief uncomfortable silence during which each of us appeared lost in our private thoughts. It was apparent Zibo-ere had told Bilflow about our strange encounter. I noticed that every now and then he looked solemnly at her, almost pleadingly. He took her hand and squeezed it, eyes misty with emotion. She returned his gaze, also squeezing his hand reassuringly and rested her head on his shoulder. The nanny soon came in, bearing Ebiere in her arms. She kissed her parents, waved to me and said 'good night!' and was carried out again. I looked over at Bilflow. Our eyes met and he heaved a deep sigh and sat up, almost reluctantly.

"O gracious! So my darling Zib, this is it? Are you sure about this, my dear?" He asked gently.

"Look, you know I respect your opinion on serious matters but I just can't help thinking whether for the first time, you may be wrong…" There was a brief silence.

"Ah my dear, don't mind me. I am just a bit overwhelmed by it all. Let's face it. By any standard, this thing you've told me. This unusual happening is, to put it delicately, unprecedented and incredible! It deserves to be published so that people will understand that supranatural occurrences are not things of the past alone."

He looked in my direction and I nodded in quiet agreement.

"Just imagine, darling," he went on.

"We are in the twentieth century and what you are saying, I mean the period you are referring to, could jolly well be some three hundred years ago! Heck, it could even be five hundred years!

This is amazing! But whatever be the case darling, you know I will always be by you to see this thing through and make whatever sense that can be made of it. You know that. So tell me what is to be done and how I can help. You know I will do anything for you don't you, my dearest?"

"Of course I do, sweetheart." Zibo-ere replied. So moved was she by her husband's impassioned speech, that she could not hold back tears. I too discreetly wiped a tear or two from my eyes. As time passed and the night wore on, it became clear to me that the night would be a long one, indeed an unending one. How could it end for us when that familiar friend sleep, had taken flight to parts unknown and not likely to return until this seemingly irresolvable puzzle could be discerned? How could it end when this long tale is yet to be unraveled and the fulfillment of a vow, taken with or without the full knowledge of its timeless implications, is still to manifest? Where and when was such a vow taken? May be I should ask which lifetime I had known Zibo-ere? I figured that knowing the answer to this last question might help untangle the mystery. I was snapped out of my mental inquisition by a deep sigh from Zibo-ere.

"Well, dearest," she whispered.

"I must go now. I do not know how this whole affair will end. All that is certain is that Layefa and I are so magnetically and intricately drawn to each other that we are convinced there is an assignment waiting for us. We are certain we know each other very well and it will be difficult to believe any argument to the contrary, despite the fact that we have just met on this earth plane. I am eternally grateful to you, my darling Bill, for your understanding and support. I wonder if I would have received the same understanding had I been married to someone else."

"An African husband would have equally understood and being supportive, I am sure," I interjected.

"Oh well, may be. Just may be! At any rate, I consider myself an extremely lucky person to be married to Bilflow. Added to this, is the blessing of being granted the ability of almost total recall of past events, possibly hundreds of years old. Do you realize, Layefa," Zibo-ere went on turning to me, "that when our story is told, if it gets told years from now, many readers will assume that the whole thing was dreamt up by some clever story teller? What fertile imagination this storyteller must have, they will exclaim! It is absolutely impossible for anyone to recall events spanning hundreds of years. It is difficult enough to vividly recall what happened five or ten years back, not to talk of hundreds of years ago. Is the person a mortal or God? Some would ask sarcastically."

Turning to Bilflow, she continued.

"But you darling, are a witness and when this affair is finally put to rest, you should tell the world about it. There may be lessons to be learnt. Tell it my dear, no matter how weird and improbable it may sound. When we leave here, Layefa and I shall go to Erere-ama, a place inhabited only by women whose task is to remain pure in mind, body and spirit for the edification of souls."

Zibo-ere had not discussed our destination with me but strangely, I felt comfortable with her statement. I knew what was necessary instinctively and explained to Bilflow that only men with a divine mission were allowed to visit Erere-ama. Such a visit would be to prepare one for some monumental assignment of great importance to the survival of mankind.

"I am sorry Bill, that you won't be able to go with us." Zibo-ere said, taking Bilflow's hand.

"You will just be transformed into a fly or some such creature if you set foot on Erere-ama! Why subject yourself to such indignity and punishment when the memory of your visit will not remain with you even after your re-transformation to a human being?" She joked.

"Pray darling, do not fret for my sake. I will be fine I promise. Take good care of Ebiere and tell her mummy has gone on an important assignment. Let my love be a source of strength for you during these uncertain times as yours will be for me. I will feel your heartbeat as you will feel mine. I love you dearly."

Deeply moved, Bilflow wanted to know exactly where this Erere- ama was but Zibo-ere told him it was impossible to reveal it. He was truly perplexed and did not know what to make of the whole thing. How could his wife, without prior notice, tell him she had to go to some mythical place that could not be revealed to him for an uncertain period of time with a man who by all accounts, was a complete stranger? He was really baffled because it just didn't make sense but being a respecter of traditions and customs and above all, his wife, he acquiesced. We assured him that real human beings who prepared a person for his or her appointed role in life inhabited the place.

As we prepared to leave, I can tell you that Bilflow was not the only apprehensive one. I too was slightly nervous. I did not have the faintest idea on how we were going to get to Erere-ama. Layefa my man, I cautioned, it is foolish to start asking yourself questions you cannot answer and raise your level of anxiety again. The die, as they say, is cast and there is no going back! Stand courageously and fulfill your mission or destiny. Draw strength from the unshakable will of Zibo-ere. Calming myself thus, I stood up and made for the door, tactfully leaving husband and wife to say their final goodbyes.

CHAPTER 4

I was waiting in the car when Zibo-ere eventually came out. She got in without a word and we drove out into the night. I headed first for my apartment so I could leave a message with a friend and next-door neighbor in case my parents or friends came looking for me. Not knowing how long I would be away, I told him to inform all callers that I had gone to a neighboring country for some specialized training. He wanted to know the particular country but I did not, indeed could not tell him. How could I when in truth, I did not know it myself! I promised I would write as soon as I settled down.

He looked pained when I refused to name my destination so I quickly apologized. I did not allow him see me off to my car in order to avoid speculations about Zibo-ere. I got into the car and we drove off. Every now and then I turned and looked at her searchingly, wondering if this adventure was not a huge mistake. Do not blame me dear readers for describing the situation as an adventure. How else could I have termed it? She squeezed my shoulder reassuringly. I kept driving, generally heading out of town but to where? I asked her if she wanted me to drive through any particular part of town but she replied in the negative.

"Just drive on and let our unseen guides take charge of the journey. Neither of us could possibly claim to know the direction to Erere-ama. I am sure that at the appropriate time, it will be revealed to us. For now, just follow your instincts. I have a feeling they will show themselves to us soon, just like the ethereal beings we used to see on the surface of the river on moonlit nights in ancient times. Do you remember that, Layefa?"

"Ehn, not quite." I replied slowly, scratching my head in an effort to remember.

"Aw come on, how can you forget the night we first saw them?" She asked, nudging my ribs gently.

"The night was almost as bright as day because of the full moon. You had joked about how you could throw a stick across the river and I dared you to do it, if you were not just boasting. You left Epele, your bosom friend and stood at the bank of the river.

When you threw the stick, it flew as if on wings and went far into the bush. You shouted in triumph, beating your chest with both hands! However, as I followed the stick with my eyes, I suddenly caught sight of a silvery white form flying across the river and I called your attention to it. Slowly, the form became more visible and took the clear form of a woman though her features were not pronounced."

As I recalled this occurrence, I also remembered my feeling of utter amazement. I originally thought it was a mermaid. Such mysterious happenings were rare in our village. Prior to this, someone had claimed to have sighted a flying entity on top of a large tree along the same river bank. According to my father, these flying things were actually beings from an unknown world. From time to time, they showed themselves to let us know that we were not the only beings in the universe. He called them oru. Anything that was beyond comprehension was usually explained away thus.

Invariably, the orukare-owei, would insist on offering sacrifices to appease the gods since it was believed that these alien appearances portended danger or evil for the village.

"There is a chill in the air, do you feel it?" Zibo-ere asked suddenly.

"Only slightly." I replied.

"Let us open our minds and hearts to receive messages from our guides." She said.

"I think they may be trying to reach us and as long as we are occupied with our own thoughts, they cannot get through. Drive without your own private thoughts from now on." I agreed and thereafter tried not to think of anything in particular and just drove on.

It may have been in the early hours of the morning when I noticed a subtle temperature change inside the car. It felt cold. I began to wonder if it was dawn already but the dashboard clock told me otherwise. Meanwhile, Zibo-ere sat so still that she could have been easily mistaken for a mannequin but for her luminous eyes which seemed to glitter. I began to have an eerie feeling of weightlessness. I could not tell whether the car was still moving on the road or in space but I knew I was still driving. Everything felt unreal, as if I was not there but I was.

Soon, we were completely enveloped in a void of whiteness. I was fully conscious, so the certainty that I was not dreaming, was not an illusion. I did not speak for fear of breaking the spell for, that was what it was, a spell!

Suddenly and inexplicably and without warning, we found ourselves in the presence of a being with an indeterminable form. I say indeterminable because we could not make out its features. It radiated light with the brilliance of a miniature sun, almost blinding but not quite.

"Welcome my children. Aado-o!" It was the gentle voice of a woman.

"Thank you. Okoide-o!" We returned, genuflecting.

Zibo-ere's eyes were wide with dawning recognition as she looked around. She reached out to me and I held her hand tightly.

"Welcome to Ere-ere-ama!" Said the same voice.

Gradually, the brilliance of the light abated and we now clearly saw the form of a five feet, nine inches tall woman of timeless beauty. She may have been between seventy and eighty years old. I looked around carefully and noticed that we were in the middle of a square, dominated by a hexagonal building which was bounded by a variety of flowers. The woman, our hostess, was standing in front of this building. "Come and have something to eat." She invited.

We dutifully followed her into the building and saw a large hall devoid of furniture.

"Please, sit down." She said indicating a side of the hall and I wondered if we were expected to sit on the bare floor. As we stood there undecided, Zibo-ere took my hand and quietly told me to sit down. We lowered ourselves to the floor and found comfortable chairs with high backs cushioning our bottoms. Where they came from and how they got there was incomprehensible to me. The hostess noticed our surprise and smiled benignly.

"Your favorite meal is on the way my children." She told us, still smiling.

As she finished speaking, a table materialized from nowhere and set itself right in front of us, just as the sweet aroma of my favorite meal assailed our nostrils. All this while, we had not seen any other person around and it bothered me a little. Glancing sideways at Zibo-ere, I noticed that she had a dreamy look in her eyes. Presently, a woman in her mid-forties, about five feet six inches tall, with chocolate colored skin came in from behind us carrying a tray containing fere, which she put on the table in front of us. Her eyes sparkled as she greeted us cheerfully.

"Sister and brother, you're welcome!" She said and left. We opened the fere and found it contained a delicious looking plantain okodo, prepared in the traditional way, with fresh fish and accompanied with palm oil. From the aroma, you did not have to taste to know that it would be delicious. Without further prompting, we devoured the food with relish. It was so delicious that other meals of okodo I had eaten before now, could at best be described as poor imitations! After the meal, we were served cool fresh palm wine.

Zibo-ere could not help asking for more as she commented that the wine must have been tapped from oil palm trees and not from raffia palm. I agreed, knowing that wine from oil palm trees usually tasted sweeter than the ones from raffia palms. It seemed to me that no palm wine could ever taste as sweet as this particular one. It definitely must contain a secret ingredient, I proclaimed! The meal over, the woman who served us came in and cleared the table. Shortly thereafter, our main hostess came over to us.

"Come now!" She said.

"You must be tired and need to rest awhile. When you have rested fully, the others will see you. Please, come with me."

We followed her outside on a short walk through a walkway along the sea shore. Mild waves lapped the shore with its pure white sand, sprinkled with different types of shells. The walkway was spotless and lined with mango and coconut trees. No house was visible, probably screened by the trees, maybe! I turned to look at Zibo-ere but she put all five fingers of her right hand to her lips, discouraging conversation. I took the hint and walked on, eyes wide with astonishment. We did not come across any other person or animal or even a fly. All was still and silent, except for the sound of lazy waves caressing the shoreline. Without warning, our hostess turned sharply to her right and we almost collided with her. Another sharp turn and there it was! A breathtakingly beautiful hexagonal structure, the color of egg yolk. It was surrounded by luxuriant bush, ablaze with colors from a variety of flowers in full bloom.

"Oh!" Zibo-ere and I exclaimed involuntarily.

"Well, Zibo-ere and Layefa, your apartments are over there."

Our hostess said, pointing straight ahead. We looked in the direction she indicated and could just make out the roof of a structure beyond the trees. "Go in now and relax. I will see you soon." With these words, she turned and left us. "Well, Layefa my dear, this is it!" Zibo-ere said, turning to me.

"Go on to your apartment and relax. You look quite nervous. Remember, all is well."

So saying, she went into hers. I stood there for a while, looking around thoughtfully before walking to mine, a few yards away. I found it strange that our hostess had known our names without being told. In fact, I wondered about a lot of things. I cannot adequately describe the interior of the apartment and the opulence that surrounded me as I opened the door and stepped across the threshold. It was like a transfiguration experience in which I had died and resurrected in heaven! I wandered from room to room. The first room I entered had lemon colored furniture and walls. The style and décor was comparable to what I imagine could be found in the homes of kings and queens. As I went from one room to the next, the story was the same. Posh interior decorations and all manner of luxury items designed for maximum pleasure and great comfort.

Beautiful paintings adorned the walls and these had a calming effect on me. I instantly felt welcomed and appreciated, a mood that pushed me into automatic relaxation mode. I counted up to six bed rooms, all exuding luxury.

There was a cozy friendliness about the place that was really inviting and I felt totally at home. As I walked around, an overwhelming feeling of exhaustion came over me. This was understandable, considering all I had been through that day. I made my way back to the first bedroom and gratefully stretched myself across the bed. As I did so, a release of tension from all parts of my body became noticeable. The feeling was blissful. It was as if I was being worked on by an invisible masseur, kneading and massaging all my tensed-up muscles. Complete pleasure took over every fiber of my being.

As I drifted off to sleep, my thoughts were of Zibo-ere and how she was taking the experience. Knowing her, I felt sure that she was coping beautifully. I soon dozed off into dreamland.

In my dream, I floated through different worlds with utmost ease and met all kinds of beings. There were happy gay ones, hostile menacing types and silent melancholic groups. They were all of different shapes and sizes. Some huge, others relatively small and yet others quite normal, like humans. These worlds were wondrous to behold and I felt intermittent flashes of hot and very cold sensations as I traversed the realms. There were flashes of brilliant blinding light one moment and a feeling of being engulfed in total darkness the next minute. I also had the distinct impression of walking on calm, tranquil seas and sometimes turbulent oceans but I was always unflustered. I had audiences with all manner of people but what was unclear was the capacity in which I held these meetings. I appeared to preside over some, while other persons presided over different events. In some instances, I joined committees to judge people. There were sitting arrangements which saw me in front seats and at times, I found myself at the back, struggling unsuccessfully to come up front. My looks too appeared disproportional as I would appear like a giant, towering above everyone with a commanding attitude at one point and then like a dwarf and insignificant looking the next moment.

All too soon or so it seemed, there was a gentle tap on my shoulder, bringing me back to earth. As I stirred and tried to clear my vision which was blurry, it was difficult to focus on the figure standing at the foot of my bed. When my eyes finally focused sufficiently, I realized that it was a person and I was in for a shock. Staring down at me was the most beautiful woman I had seen for some time and I had seen quite a few lately. As I tried to make out who the angelic specimen could be, she called my name softly. I sat up and shook my head as if still a little groggy with sleep and then, I got another surprise.

"Why, Zibo-ere, it's you! But… but you look so…so different, so heavenly, like… like an angel!"

I was confused. True enough the woman really looked like Zibo-ere to me, except that she certainly looked more radiant and ethereal, a trait that was not as pronounced in Zibo-ere as it seemed now. She just stood there and smiled gently at me.

"I am not Zibo-ere, my dear." She laughed softly.

"I am Zibobra, her twin."

Her twin? I was more confused now. I did not know Zibo-ere had a twin sister. Seeing the look of consternation on my face, she stretched out her hand and I took it. She pulled me out of bed and led me to a couch at a corner of the room and I sat down gratefully.

"Everything will become perfectly clear to you in due course," she told me.

"I have been assigned to be your guide and companion for the period of your stay here. In a few hours, there will be a meeting of elders. Zibo-ere will be in attendance at the meeting but you cannot attend because you are not fully prepared yet. It is my duty to assist in clearing whatever fog is obscuring your sense of perception and adaptability, after which your system will be light enough to be accommodated."

She stopped briefly to see how I was taking it.

"If you look around, you will notice that everything you could possibly need to make your stay comfortable has been provided. From now on, there will be no need to call on anyone for anything that you desire. That you desire it, is enough for it to appear. So, be careful and exercise extreme care and discipline in your thoughts.

This privilege provided you by Temearau is not to be misused. As much as you have earned it, misuse can lead to its Withdrawal. This is a good reason to reorder priorities."

I listened attentively as she tutored me on what was expected of me. As I listened, I could not imagine what I had done to deserve such favor and I ventured to ask her. She did not immediately answer my question. Instead, she invited me for a walk. I got up silently and went outside with her. I was surprised to see that it was still day light. We had been in this place for some time now and had even slept, a sleep, which I was sure, must have been a long one. So I had expected it to be dark outside or at least, dusk.

"It is still daylight, how come?" I asked, unable to hold back my curiosity.

"Patience!" She implored.

"Let us sit over there."

She indicated a row of comfortable garden chairs in a garden, hedged by a closely cropped row of queen of the night flowers, their enchanting fragrance filling the air. Idly, I envisioned how strong the scent would be at night, if it was this strong during the day. Anyone with knowledge of flowers knows that the fragrance from queen of the night flowers is usually strongest at night.

"I assure you, all will soon become clear to you and in some cases, without explanation from anyone," Zibobra emphasized. We moved over and sat in the chairs, complete with footstools. They were even more comfortable than expected and before long, I had that sensation of being massaged again! I sat back, stretched out my legs and relaxed. Soon, an inexplicable feeling of reinvigoration enveloped me. I felt so positively buoyant that I had the feeling of floating in the air! I felt like someone without bones in his body. My mood and feeling was such that I would not have been surprised if I had developed wings and flown to parts unknown! Zibobra looked at me and smiled knowingly. She began to speak contemplatively.

"When Zibo-ere and I decided that we would be born together, we could not make up our minds on which part of earth to go to." Though sited beside me, it seemed as if she was talking from afar.

"It was important that we be born in an area where we could carry out our assignment of saving souls, averting evil and creating happiness without let or hindrance. We looked over the entire world and decided on a riverine community far from big towns and cities. Then, we had to choose our parents carefully. It was imperative that we had parents who were simple but courageous, upright and spiritual. Even though we were able to find two such persons who were ideal for us, bringing them together and making them attractive to each other was another issue that had to be overcome. We finally succeeded and they got married." With a little smile playing around her luscious lips, she went on.

"Now, in those days, it was a tough battle to be born as twins in that part of the world. The people were very superstitious, attributing every new or unusual event or phenomenon to evil forces of the universe. They were more at home with simple and familiar occurrences. Giving birth to a set of twins was certainly not familiar. Our mother suffered minimal labour pains. In fact, she delivered us without assistance and only drank a concoction prepared from local herbs to make her strong."

Zibobra paused in her monologue and looked at me to see if I was following and probably, to give me an opportunity to ask questions if I had any. I had been listening with rapt attention and as I did not seem to have any questions, she continued.

"The village high priestess was informed of our birth and she immediately ordered that we be taken to her shrine and sacrificed to the gods to purify the village and cleanse it of the abomination. Ordinarily and according to tradition, our parents would have put us in a small basket and drowned us but the priestess had to be obeyed. For some peculiar reason, the ritual executioner was reluctant to carry out the sacrifice so he devised a way to save us. He arranged for our parents to go on self-exile with us to a tiny fishing village far away. This they did, thus saving our lives."

At this point, she stopped and requested for refreshments, which consisted of a variety of fresh fruits and a plateful of dried processed cassava. As promised earlier, these materialized from nowhere and placed on a stool in front of me before I knew it. I must have been hungrier than I thought for, I ate the food ravenously. I had almost finished eating everything before I realized that Zibobra was not eating and shamefacedly asked her why.

"I was waiting for you to invite me. In this place, it is of utmost importance to care about the needs of each other. It is only through such symbiotic relationships that the harmony and sanctity you find here is maintained and sustained through time."

As she finished speaking, her fruit bowl also appeared. I noticed that the fruits were dipped in honey and were cut into different shapes with tiny sticks stuck in each piece. She ate silently, picking them one at a time with the sticks and chewing each mouthful thoughtfully before swallowing. It was as if she was trying to teach me eating etiquette. I suspect that she must have noticed how quickly I ate in my hunger-induced haste. This was another lesson I had to learn. She resumed her narration after the refreshments.

"For the first two years of our lives, we were reared in secrecy. Our parents were afraid that the village where they were in exile would also find twins abominable. Our mother hardly ever went out of the hut we lived in. She was always with us. When we eventually ventured outside a little after the age of two, we were looked upon as goddesses, possibly because we were identical both in facial features and complexion. Our skin was very light and we were extremely beautiful, with very long luxuriant black hair. People brought offerings from both far and near for the twin 'goddesses' and soon the status of our parents improved. There was hardly anything we could do as children when people took us for goddesses and brought offerings. However, as we grew older, we made our parents understand our displeasure at being regarded as goddesses. We were determined to put a stop to it." After a short pause, she continued.

"The opportunity came through a dramatic turn of events when we were in our early teens. It was on a market day and a group of over-zealous devotees had gathered in front of our hut to present offerings as usual. Our mother came out to decline the offerings and inform them that we were not goddesses. She therefore advised them to go home and seek other gods or goddesses to worship. The leader of the group, a short pot-bellied man with bald patches all over his small head would hear none of that and swore at her. The sound of his swearing brought us out to the front yard from the cooking area behind the hut where we were boiling plantain. On sighting us, they all fell to their knees and did obeisance. Their leader, who was also an orukare-owei, went on to express his displeasure at our mother's rejection of their offerings. Without uttering a word, Zibo-ere and I linked hands, stood directly in front of the priest and pointed at a big tree across the river. In a flash, the priest found himself sitting atop a high branch of that same tree! We only brought him down after he earnestly pleaded and promised not to worship us again. Word soon went round all the villages and worshiping us as goddesses stopped instantly." She paused and looked at me.

"I will stop here for now as we are due to meet Zibo-ere and others soon. I shall complete the narration at another convenient time."

So saying, she got up and indicated that I follow. I got up and walked beside her keeping a little distance between us to avoid contact. I didn't want to touch her by mistake, just in case it was taboo!

CHAPTER 5

"We do not know day and night here as it is in your world on earth," Zibobra told me as we walked on.

I had no idea where we were going but that did not really bother me. I just walked beside her knowing that the next agenda would unfold soon enough.

"When our weather dims, gets cloudy or dusky, it means there's disharmony in our system and we immediately realign our thought processes to bring back balance."

"Really!" I exclaimed not too surprised.

I had since concluded that everything in this place was extraordinarily different from the vibrations of earth.

"Yes, Layefa, our world was created to be of great benefit and assistance to us and the least we can do is obey the laws which guarantee our sustenance. Here we are!" She said suddenly, ending the conversation as we came upon a small group of ladies. They were about six in all and had obviously been waiting for us. They fell silent and looked at me curiously, smiling. Zibobra introduced me to them and they formed a circle around me.

"Welcome, our friend and brother!" They said in unison. Though young girls, they had the look of maturity that made it difficult to place their ages with any degree of accuracy but twenty to twenty-five may not be too far-fetched. Their apparels were fascinating but familiar. The traditional 'up-and-down,' a blouse worn over an ankle-length wrapper and another wrapper, wrapped over the blouse at the waist, extending downwards to just below the knees. The outfits were made of a material that looked like a combination of velvet, lace and damask and all in the now familiar lemon color. Their long hair was plaited in the traditional style with black thread and their feet were encased in slippers of lemon colored cloth material.

Zibobra indicated that I sit on the ground, a lush green lawn in the center of the circle. I looked down at the grass and reluctantly lowered myself. It felt so soft and comfortable as if I was sitting on a padded sofa in a living room so I had to look down again to see and confirm that I was actually sitting on grass. I was! Amazing, I muttered. But then again, I was surprised at my surprise! The girls also lowered themselves gracefully onto the lawn, this time, forming a semicircle in front of me while Zibobra remained standing next to me. She gestured at one of them and the lady in question smiled brightly at me and began to speak.

"Layefa, our brother, we are all very excited to welcome you to Erere-ama. You are not aware but we have been working with you internally and even physically at times, all through the ages. Our assistance to you in every way was to ensure that you always did the right thing in order not to jeopardize your chances of fulfilling your destiny."

I looked at her soberly, as she continued.

"It has been quite challenging and at times, it looked like you were bent on self-destruction, no matter how much we tried to distract or redirect you."

She stopped talking and all the others nodded in agreement. Zibobra looked at another one of the girls and inclined her head at her. The girl in question looked at me with an enchanting smile.

"Our dear Layefa, we greet you! When we voluntarily took up the assignment of monitoring you, we were quite certain that you would ultimately triumph, no matter the obstacles and trials that you may face. Along the way, you cried out to your guardians on many occasions for help. By the grace of the Creator, we were always around and responded promptly to your pleas. Though at times, you forgot your power of free will and blamed other things and other people for your mistakes and shortcomings, we were confident that sooner or later, realization would dawn on you. Truly, you finally realized that all humans were created with the power of discretion and volition. The responsibility to critically weigh choices open to you before embarking on any action invariably rests squarely with you. The Creator put in all of us the ability to look after ourselves, to be able to hold our own and to save ourselves from all harm, physical and spiritual. Indeed, we are created complete." she stated firmly.

I pondered her words, reflecting deeply on the implication and import. I looked from one lovely face to the other. Something had bothered me as I listened to the speakers but I resisted the impulse to ask questions, at least for the moment. It seemed that every one of them was to make her own contribution to the 'lecture session.' Zibobra soon looked at another 'sister' and that was a signal for her to begin. However just as she was about to start speaking, Zibo-ere, looking radiant came into the arena. Six equally beautiful ladies, all similarly attired like the ones around me accompanied her. I sucked in my breath unconsciously. There was a happy chorus of 'welcome!' from the girls sitting around me.

"Oh sister Zibo-ere, welcome! Welcome!" Was the chorus as they rose as one and elatedly embraced her, one after the other.

After the greetings, Zibo-ere turned to her twin Zibobra and they locked themselves in a tight warm embrace. All the girls looked on with delight. On my part, it was awe the scene evoked as I stared at them from my sitting position on the grass. Curiously, there was a peculiar brightness around the two. Thousands of multi-colored butterflies fluttered around them. They were of course oblivious to the happenings around them. The duo separated briefly to look at each other at arm's length, laughed joyously and embraced again. At last, they sat down together with the other girls. Ziboere looked at me and flashed a dazzling smile. At a signal from Zibobra again, the 'sister' that was interrupted by Zibo-ere's arrival began her speech.

"Dear Layefa, once you became aware of the innate strength and discretionary ability you possessed, in addition to the abundant possibilities open to you, there was no holding you back. You excelled and with this excellence came opportunities hitherto unavailable to you. We were always with you and not surprisingly, you won the confidence of so many people. When you were made the leader of your community during your third incarnation, everyone was happy because the choice was unanimous. You did well during the initial years of your reign and all was well in your community. You always listened to the wise counsel of your elders. Your first wife, a very enlightened woman was also supportive and gave you good advice. After about five years of this idyllic existence, you began to stray from your upright ways. You abandoned the counsel of the elders for that of immature peers and even began to indulge in unwholesome amorous relationships and drunken orgies. You became self-righteous and made wrong decisions that were disastrous for your community. Opposition to your style of rulership soon emerged but you were iron-handed and despotic, jailing and most times, killing those who opposed you. The more dictatorial you became the more strident the opposition. It was soon obvious to us that the end was near for you. Predictably, another person of stronger character was chosen as a replacement and you were banished from the community. You later died in exile, depressed and bitter. Your death was difficult and painful to us because you did not recapture the innocence of your youth before transiting, a requirement for the fulfillment of your destiny. Instead, you had built up a pitiable veil of darkness around not only yourself but those you loved. Nevertheless, we were on hand to welcome you with our true and pure love when you passed on." So saying, she smiled at me and sat down.

I was thoroughly dismayed. My mouth hung open in amazement as she concluded her story. I could not help pointing at myself.

"Me?" I asked after a little pause. "The person you just talked about was me?"

I looked from one beautiful face to the other, confused. All heads nodded in agreement. Indeed, it was me. There was no mistake about it. I could not believe that I, Layefa, considered by friends to be just part of the citizenry and born to parents that were quite ordinary had actually been a great ruler hundreds of years ago! The more I thought about it the more befuddled I became and all the recent happenings around me did not help matters either. I shook my head from side to side a few times in an effort to clear the cobwebs in my brain. Then I felt the cool, almost electrifying but reassuring touch of Zibo-ere's hand on my shoulder. I looked at her and put my cheek against her hand getting what little comfort and reassurance I could from it. Hunger gnawed at my intestines and with the thought that I was actually hungry, came the sweet aroma of delicious food wafting through the air. I remembered what Zibobra told me. Soon, assorted foods were in front of us. The girls opened them with happy exclamations. "Delicious food is here, brother Layefa!"

"This is a banquet!" I said to Zibo-ere, all tension gone.

"Yes Layefa. I am sure the food will be tasty, just like our first meal here. Go ahead and eat while I join Zibobra."

We all ate in silence but with enjoyment. Soul stirring music filtered through the air. We ate slowly, ever so slowly, savoring the delicious taste of the food and the soothing effect of the music. Birds and butterflies circled and fluttered elegantly above and around us. It was all so enchanting and surreal like a fairyland and in all honesty, I did not want the scene to fade away.

CHAPTER 6

With the meal over, Zibobra asked if everyone would like light entertainment or continue with 'discussion on Layefa,' as she put it. "O music! Let's dance!" Was the unhesitating and unanimous answer. It would appear that democracy had some foothold in the place! Zibobra had to go with the majority decision.

"Very well, then! Maestro, come forth and transport us to higher heights with your music. Accompany oh beings of eternal light, the maestro and carry us on wings of total joy. Come, oh come, my friends!"

As she finished making this proclamation, what can only be described as music of the spheres, drifted up to us and slowly increased in tempo. Sprinkles of confetti began to fall and a kaleidoscope of colors formed around us. The weather dimmed appropriately to give full effect. Then the maestro, a plump lady of medium height with silvery-white hair and stately bearing entered, playing an instrument which was neither a guitar nor a harp. A teenage girl played the drums with gusto. I was more interested in the music than the instrument that produced it anyway. As we applauded, a bevy of young beauties attired in traditional costumes of yellow blouses over multicolored wrappers tied at the waist streamed in. They sang with such warmth and joy that we listened first with a sense of awe, then with all our beings. We applauded enthusiastically when they stopped singing. One of the singers stepped up to Zibo-ere and said.

"A special song for you our most precious sister. Hold my hand and join if you like or just listen."

I watched amused, as Zibo-ere followed the girl who began to sing, slowly at first. Then as the singing gathered momentum she disengaged her hand from the singer's and began to sway in rhythm with the drumming. This developed into a graceful and absorbing dance that moved almost everyone to join in. At a point, she slowed more or less to a halt and beckoned on me to join her. Like one hypnotized, I got up slowly and took her outstretched hands.

It was pure magic when we started dancing. With synchronized steps and movement, it seemed like something we had rehearsed hundreds of times before. Everything seemed so familiar, so perfect! Soon, other dancers stopped dancing and all eyes were riveted on us. Our dancing increased in pace and climaxed as the drumming reached a crescendo. Everyone surrounded us hugging, laughing and applauding delightedly as the dance ended.

I frankly did not know I could dance like that! Everything was nouvelle to me and yet it seemed natural.

I was really happy. Next, Zibo-ere was asked to do a solo.

"Me? But I can't sing my sister." She said lamely turning to Zibobra, who was smiling.

"Of course you can my dear sister. You can sing. Do, sing for us!" Zibobra told her, matter-of-factly.

At this, Zibo-ere, seemingly resigned to her fate, opened her mouth and began to sing. What we heard instantly induced silence. It was the most soulful and melodious rendition of any song I had ever heard. Everyone gazed at her in admiration. At a point, what looked like showers of dry white paint covered the air, falling like snowflakes on her glistening face as she looked towards the sky.

It was quite an experience I tell you. At the end of her performance, there was thunderous ovation. It was so loud that one could only conclude that there must have been an unseen audience present too! Just the few of us assembled there could not have produced such resonance. At long last, she thanked the maestro and her team and bid them 'baiyo-o!' They departed singing a quietly haunting melody, a fitting close to a wonderful entertainment.

With the happy vibrations of their departing song still palpable in the air, Zibobra announced that Zibo-ere and I were to be taken before the welcoming mother, our chief hostess and her council. Layefa old fellow this is it, I told myself a little apprehensively. Zibo-ere, sensing my nervousness took my hand.

"Layefa my dear, have you still not come to terms with our situation?" She asked gently.

"Please don't mind me. I guess I am still overwhelmed by all that has been happening. I am just a thick-headed fool!"

"Oh no, you are not!" She said.

"It is all a delayed reaction. Your system is taking a bit longer to get attuned to the reality of things, that is all." She squeezed my hand reassuringly.

"I agree with you my sister." Chipped in Zibobra.

It was at that point I noticed that the others had left, leaving the three of us to continue our experience. They had slipped away so quietly that one would think they just disappeared into thin air! Zibobra read my unasked question correctly and told me that the mothers wanted us to visit them alone.

"Even I cannot accompany you this time. Just follow that blue bird hovering above you." We looked up at the little blue bird fluttering its beautiful wings above us.

"It will lead you to your destination. Just remember that my love, our love, follows you everywhere and it follows you now."

So saying, she pushed us gently forward, towards the hovering bird and then vanished or so it seemed. We looked at each other in silent wonder then turned and followed the bird which was waiting patiently. I noticed as I looked closely at Zibo-ere that she looked so much younger than before. I could not tell if I too looked younger.

"Yes Layefa, it is impossible for us to pass through this experience and still look and sound the same. I perceived the question in your mind as you looked at me. Ha, don't look so surprised! It is all part of the experience."

I gave her a peculiar look when she said this. How did she know the question in my mind? I must confess, since the beginning of this adventure, she appeared to have more readily come to grips with our situation than me. The way she danced, sang and generally understood our circumstance much better than I did, sort of gave me the impression that she had more 'powers.'

"We have so much to discuss Layefa but it is not yet time," she said.

"We are not quite harmonized mentally and spiritually and that must happen before the culmination of what I will call our work."

All this while, we were following the little bird which would fly forward a little ahead and wait for us to catch up with it before flying forward again. We had just turned a corner when we heard a familiar voice.

"Oh, here they are!" The voice said behind us. Turning around, we saw our hostess, the welcoming mother who had received us when we first arrived. This time she was accompanied by five women similarly of timeless beauty and of the same age bracket, between seventy and eighty years. They looked youngish with smooth faces bereft of wrinkles.

"Okoisine-O!" We greeted, genuflecting.

"Seri, awou-ama!" They replied, smiling.

"Come children, follow me!" Said the leader.

We obeyed and walked along, followed closely by the five women. She stopped at a clearing already arranged with strange looking chairs, yellow three-legged contraptions, armless and without cushions. The backrests appeared to be made of fine feathery material. Seven chairs in all were arranged in a semi-circle and the welcoming mother, being the leader, made straight for the one in the middle and sat down. The other women took their seats, leaving the one to the immediate right of the welcoming mother vacant.

"Come children stand before us over there." Said the leader, pointing to the center of the semi-circle. We moved to the spot indicated and stood with our arms by our sides.

"Now, look around you and tell us what you see." She instructed. With a little laugh, I looked around carefully and cleared my throat.

"I see a great bush around the clearing," I began.

"I also see very bright yellow flowers next to your chairs and very many butterflies pecking at the flowers. Over there behind you are Indian bamboos with branches shading you and forming what looks like a star. To the left of Zibo-ere is a very unusual looking tree. It has no branches and is smaller than all the others in the area and has a concentration of blazing red and pink flowers at its tip. I can also see numerous birds circling the clearing. That is all I see." Then it was Zibo-ere's turn to state what she had noticed.

"I can hear the soft sound of waves lapping against the shore," Zibo-ere began. "Looking carefully around, I noticed a swamp surrounding this clearing. Over there to the right is a pond filled with flowering lilies as well as fishes. The wild flowers a little to the left behind Layefa are bright, fragrant and appear to appeal to the birds more than other flowers. I also noticed a swarm of busy bees below the higher branches of the trees to my right that are certain to be producing honey. Several odd shaped mushrooms surround the clearing at the far-right corner. Their colors range from pure white to light brown to silvery gray. This is all, my mothers." She concluded.

I was astounded at her observational abilities and concluded that if this had been a test, she would have scored higher marks than me. Once again, it occurred to me that Zibo-ere must have great extra-sensory powers.

"Children!" Called the welcoming mother.

"Now that we know how you see your environment, we are ready to begin. Zibo-ere, you will now undress Layefa and drop all his clothes on the ground at his feet."

Wonder of wonders! I was to be undressed in front of all these women? I remarked, strictly to myself mind you! Zibo-ere turned to me and proceeded to undress me. To my surprise, I was not at all as uncomfortable as I thought I would be. In fact, I was so at ease that I felt no embarrassment as she removed my last article of clothing! Strange I tell you!

"Come and sit by me, child." The welcoming mother said to Zibo-ere, who quickly obliged.

I assumed that I was stark naked, my clothes having been removed by Zibo-ere as directed. Involuntarily but quite naturally, I discreetly brought down my hands to cover my genitals. But instead of touching bare flesh, I felt a filmy substance and quickly looked down to discover that I was not at all naked but clothed in a fine silky body hugging suit. I noticed all this with a sense of detachment, like I was observing or viewing someone else's body.

"Now Layefa my child, do sit down and we shall begin as requested by you and Zibo-ere in times past."

I looked around and since there was no other vacant seat, I made to sit on the ground but found my bottom cushioned by a quarter-stool, which sprang from the ground. I was now beginning to get used to these strange manifestations.

"Before we begin," she continued.

"Look deep into my eyes and try to recall who I am. Draw strength and inspiration from the inexhaustible love you already feel in the air. Look deep Layefa and touch and feel what is offered by us all. You freely requested and we freely accepted your request for support."

As she finished speaking, my eyes were drawn to hers and I looked into her eyes with all the intensity I could muster, as suggested. Gradually, as if entranced, a feeling of lightness, followed by drowsiness came over me. This state felt so agreeable that I just wanted to sink into a deep sleep from which I would not want to wake up in a hurry. It was difficult to tell if my eyes remained open all this time but suddenly I shouted in recognition.

"Okosu-ere! Is that you over there? Okosu-ere! This is magnificent! O, fantastic my very dear mother!

"Yes it is me, dear Layefa! It is me. I am elated that you can now progress. I told you that I would keep my side of our little bet because you were such a dynamic and thoughtful person.

You had the heart of a child, uncomplicated, unsullied and uncluttered. You loved so freely. I told you that if at all possible, it would be done, no matter how many life times it took."

All I could do was repeat her name over and over, followed by our traditional greeting.

"Okoide-O! Okoide, Okosu-ere!" I was overwhelmed by this recognition but Okosu-ere directed her assistants to proceed with the exercise.

"Yes! Yes!" All agreed. "Let us begin, Okosu-ere."

"Then let the music play. Beat the instruments musians and come forth O dancing girls!" Okosu-ere ordered.

As I watched, indeed, as all present watched, lithe and agile dancers seemingly jumped out of the surrounding bushes into the open space. They danced with passion, carrying trays laden with objects I could not make out. The music was fierce and intense, coming fast from the direction of the Indian bamboos. The dancing girls, three in number, danced round me and then one by one, dropped the trays at my feet. They then danced over to where the mothers sat and knelt briefly before them. They got up and invited Zibo-ere to join in the dancing.

"Come now sister, the hour has come. Come and do your duty as requested by you hundreds of years ago. Fulfill sister, your sacred obligation. Come now!" They chanted.

She rose slowly, ever so slowly and raised her arms as if in prayer, then broke into a wild dance. The music became even more piercing and fast-paced as Zibo-ere, surrounded by the dancing girls danced around the clearing several times. In the midst of the dancing, I noticed thick smoke coming out from a hole in the ground. Soon after, Okosu-ere stood up fully erect and raised her right hand. At this signal, the music and dancing stopped abruptly. She moved deliberately to Zibo-ere and enveloped her in a tight, long embrace, eyes closed. At last she released her, took a step back, looked at me and in a thunderous voice made this solemn declaration.

"I, Okosu-ere, now call on you O timeless Temearau, creator of all there is and ever will be, to witness this ceremony of rejuvenation of your children. Oh, sisters and mothers of years gone by, tune into our space and witness for all time, the ceremony of this day. Oh mothers here seated, add your voices to mine and bring forth our mighty custodians of virtue. Rise now and call forth!" She commanded. The assembled mothers as one, raised their voices and chanted.

"Mighty custodians of virtue, we invoke your presence. Oh mighty custodians of life, come and preside at this ceremony. Oh mighty custodians of light come and be our guests. Oh Temearau, shower us with your blessings. Oh Temearau, bless your children Zibo-ere and Layefa, as they fulfill their sacred duty." Immediately after this intense invocation, they called out.

"Zibo-ere! Zibo-ere! Zibo-ere! Layefa! Layefa! Layefa! Bring your wishes to Temearau as we present you before her." Zibo-ere turned to me.

"Give me your hand, soul of my soul." She said this so softly that I had to strain my ears to hear her. I extended my hand and she took it. Together, palms raised high above our heads, we began to implore.

"O Temearau! Receive our sincere words and bless us. Oh, take us to your timeless and glorious sphere. We open our souls to you. Reinvigorate us. Recreate us. Oh, create us anew. Accept Oh Temearau, our offer of self-sacrifice. Strengthen us with your eternal power. Make us your permanent messengers of peace and love. We pledge our love, our truth, ourselves and our souls. Accept Oh Temearau, these words of supplication and bless us. We consecrate ourselves to you. We open our souls to receive your blessings now."

By the time we ended our supplication and became aware of activities around us, the entire arena was parked with women in different colorful traditional attires.

CHAPTER 7

The original team led by Okosu-ere solemnly presented Zibo-ere with a glittering knife taken from one of the trays left at my feet by the dancers and charged her to use it well.

"Now proceed with your task my beloved, as we stand by to support you." Said one of the mothers.

By this time, Zibo-ere and I were standing in the center of the clearing. She touched my forehead with the knife and in a flash, I found myself floating in the air! But wait a minute, my physical body was still standing in the same place! Have I become two persons in one or what, was my immediate thought.

Shortly thereafter, Okosu-ere retrieved the knife from Zibo-ere and presented her with a heavier knife of pure silver. She did this as solemnly as the first time. All the mothers quickly surrounded us and my right hand was held by one of them and the left by another. Zibo-ere touched the crown of my head lightly with the tip of the knife and my body fell to the ground in slow motion. I was not apprehensive, scared or worried about my safety all through this process as I watched from high above the heads of everybody. As a matter of fact, I viewed everything as a detached on-looker. I was present but not really there. It was all very intriguing. Everyone keenly witnessed the exercise including the un-seen guests invited by Okosu-ere to be eternal witnesses to the fulfillment of our avowed destiny.

Presently, Okosu-ere and her team raised their arms up in quiet solicitation then spread them out, palms up and eyes closed. As they did this, subtle ethereal music permeated the air. All was quiet except for this insidious music. Then the most fragrant scent of roses, gardenias and lavenders wafted through the air. Zibo-ere soon broke the silence by starting a high-pitched song in praise of Temearau.

"O Temearau e deba mo-O. Temearau ede ba mo-O. O Creator you are great! O Creator you are great!" She sang melodiously and ecstatically, looking at my body now neatly arranged in the basket! Gradually, my body became engulfed in a mist. Zibo-ere continued her song alone for about five minutes before everyone joined in, in perfect harmony and rhythm. The song they sang was reflective and prayerful. The singing continued for some time and almost without being noticed, the mist cleared. Loo! Standing erect and looking noble and extremely handsome was my humble self, Layefa! The two 'selves' now fused into one perfect whole. Yes, there I was with a joyous countenance, looking around the gathered assemblage of graceful women. I felt neither shock nor surprise at this transformation, as if it was a normal thing. Shouts of joy from all present rent the air.

"Wuwu, wuwu-u, wuwu-u-u! Ebimo-O! Ebimo-O wuu wu!"

They shouted and laughed and hugged each other excitedly. Finally, Okosu-ere clapped her hands for attention and all fell silent.

"Oh Temearau, I greet you with all my being for this day! Erere-ama has once again received your unbounded blessings. We shall forever sing your praises. Okoide, Temearau! A million greetings are too few to express our gratitude. Please accept our collective greetings."

"Okoide-O Temearau! Okoide!" Everyone chorused, kneeling. Okosu-ere turned and beckoned to me and Zibo-ere.

"It is done my dear children. Come away and sleep awhile. There is still much to learn and see and know before you depart." She then turned to the other women now seated.

"Mothers and Zibobra, lead them home in peace."

Those summoned surrounded us, chatting in subdued tones.

This time, they took us into a different building.

"Sleep well." They said to us and left but Zibobra remained and showed us to our different rooms.

"That is your room my sister," she said to Zibo-ere pointing at a door, "and that is yours Layefa." She inclined her head towards another door not far from the first one, then took leave of us.

We both entered our separate rooms as soon as she left. I must have been fatigued without knowing it because, within minutes, I was fast asleep and dreaming. In my dream, I was taught many things about creation. I crisscrossed different worlds viewing diverse life processes. There appeared to be life forms everywhere I looked. There was life and energy permeating everywhere and everything. It seemed so natural to me. Interestingly, I saw Ziboere and Zibobra traveling the worlds too! We were both aware of each other's presence in the various planes where we journeyed but did not communicate verbally. It was as though we had different instructors teaching the same subjects but in their own special ways.

I woke up feeling energized and happy. I sat up and pondered my dream. I became intuitively aware that Zibo-ere was also awake. Though we were in different rooms, I knew my feeling was right. Getting out of bed, I stretched and decided to have a little chat with her. I went outside and saw her seated in a garden beside the building where we slept, playing with some animals and birds, talking to them and laughing. When she saw me she waved, inviting me to join her.

"Come over dear one. We have been waiting for you. Let us eat with these friends of mine." She said, pointing to the animals. I sat beside her gratefully and suddenly realized how hungry I was. I greeted the animals, stroking as many as came close to me. They were wild but obviously harmless, the first I had seen since we came to Erere-ama. The sweet aroma of a prepared meal drifted to us and my stomach rumbled. Soon, Zibobra came, followed by another woman carrying a tray bearing covered dishes. She invited us over to where chairs had been arranged and the woman carrying the tray placed it on a low stool and left.

"This, my beloved ones, is a celebration meal comprising okodo, pulou-feyai and lufeyai, all prepared with sea food. We shall eat together from the same bowl as a sign of our continuing love, fraternity and solidarity. We shall eat with our fingers as a mark of humility and simplicity of heart." Zibo-ere agreed and said our rebirth at Erere-ama could not be taken lightly.

"Zibo-ere, you have just echoed my thoughts. I agree totally." I said.

"Let's eat then and let the maestro also give us food for the soul!

We must take care of both," Zibobra said, laughing. The sound of soft music drifted over to us immediately thereafter and we began to eat. Our conversation during the meal was minimal, allowing the music talk to us in its soothing and uplifting language. We lingered over the meal, taking our time and savoring every mouthful. We were blissful and contented. The weather as expected, was mild and very comfortable, indeed perfect. I remembered what Zibobra told me the first time I asked whether there was no night or day in Erere-ama so I was not surprised that the weather was perfect. We all felt pure and without blemish.

Oh Temarau I prayed silently, let this day never end. Let this happy occasion continue forever! Prayer or no prayer, the meal had to end and so it did. The woman who served us came and cleared the plates and we settled down in loving companionship, with silent soothing music still in the background.

"Zibo-ere, I now understand what you were telling me when we first arrived Erere-ama. You were so confident and sure when you said that soon my eyes would fully open."

"Of course I was sure, very sure that by the time we finished with the peletuwo ceremony of rebirth, the remaining 'scales' would fall off from your eyes."

"The invincibility clause in your vow made it necessary for you to pass through several lifetimes before becoming thoroughly 'cured' for its actualization my dear ones," Zibobra reminded us.

My memory by this time, was fully restored and served me well. I distinctly remembered being told by Okosu-ere that it took ages for her to achieve immortality. By the same token, if Zibo-ere and I wanted to be immortal, it would also take us many lifetimes of dedicated work to achieve it. We were so sure of ourselves then that we readily made the commitment. Okosu-ere had counseled that the responsibilities were enormous. She also said absolute purity of thoughts and love for all things and beings was imperative for ultimate success. She had reminded us that once the vow was made, it remained irrevocable for all time. Zibo-ere I now recalled, had undertaken to help me at great risk to herself because if I failed to meet my side of the commitment, she would be dragged down with me. I had a dense nature then and it took me longer to discern spiritual truths. Fortunately though, once I had grasped the truth it stuck and I was more resolute. I turned to her and asked if she thought there could ever be such a bond as ours, so selfless and unconditional? She smiled broadly and shook her head.

"Dearest Layefa, souls that are bonded in love have similar experiences like we've had but paths can never be the same. Remember that Zibobra had never left me and her constant invisible companionship strengthened and supported our love, ensuring that it never waned. Our love is pure and untainted and has remained so because it is a soul love. Our two souls met and fused in the higher realms. We felt and Zibobra agreed with us that in order to sustain the light of this love and ensure that it burned continually, we had to make the sacrifice of having other physical partners. This of course, was out of respect for the Creator's plan of repopulating the world again and again. It is not certain though, whether there may come a time when our relationship could move into a different sphere or phase. It all depends on the soul gains and benefits for all concerned."

Zibo-ere, you're perfectly right," I cut in.

"Okosu-ere specifically admonished us not to ignore the Creator's will. She told us to align our thoughts, words and deeds to the Creator's will."

"Exactly!" Zibo-ere agreed."

"Okosu-ere also told us that Temearau talks to us all the time but she does not force us to listen or take note. The free will she has granted her creatures implies that the effort is theirs to make if they want to learn. Do you remember the night she gave us that admonition?" I asked drawing her close to me.

I no longer had fears about our physical closeness. The knowledge that the spiritual nature of our love would remain no matter what, boosted my confidence no end. I also now realized why

I was so afraid to touch or become too close to her when we first rediscovered ourselves. I had sub-consciously known that I was not spiritually 'clean' enough to be close to her. I also marveled at the depth of love existing between the sisters, Ziboere and Zibobra. It was as though their umbilical cords, having been severed from their mother at birth, reconnected within them spiritually, becoming an everlasting link through time and space even while one was 'dead' and the other 'alive.'

Their ability to look out for each other while in different dimensions and spheres of existence is one of Temearau's mysteries which will always inspire awe. Who can truly understand Temearau's world and its incomprehensibility, I dare ask? No being in all universes, I dare conclude. Take the pele-tuwo transformation ceremony I had just undergone for instance, not only have my spiritual eyes become fully open but I have also become invincible, almost immortal. For as long as I do not get caught in the trap of vanity and foolishness, no other mortal being can do me harm. In addition, I would now be able to read the thoughts of other humans and any other being within my immediate environment and beyond. This no doubt puts a stupendous responsibility on me but I do not mind at all. It was because of all these that Zibo-ere and I had to pass through several life times before achieving this feat. A mortal being unprepared by time and experiences can never attain what we have now achieved. The beauty of it all is that it is open to all who are prepared to make the sacrifice. I was jolted by the sound of Zibobra's voice calling my attention to something.

"Is it not so, dearest Layefa?" she repeated.

"Oh pardon me, Zibobra. I did not hear you. What did you say?"

"Aaboo Layefa!" She laughed.

"Are you already out of here? Never mind though, I understand. I was just telling you and Zibo-ere to prepare for departure. We shall all miss you in a way because henceforth, our contact shall be only spiritual. Though in a sense, we will always be together.

All the same, it still does not prevent us from missing you just a little! The work you have to do from now on will be of crucial importance to the world and the lessons you must teach, even more so. Look to the right, the mothers are already gathered and to the front, the teachers of light have also gathered. Turn around and see the singing and dancing girls behind you. Look to your left and see the eternal friends of wisdom gather. Now dear Zibo-ere, go to them and receive your embrace of pure love with its ever expanding radiations of peace and goodwill to all. You too dear Layefa, go and receive your embrace which only the few who are considered worthy are ever given."

Busting with a feeling of immeasurable affection, we moved from group to group receiving our life sustaining embraces of love. As we did so, poignant music filled the air and the sweet fragrances of unknown wild flowers or divinely prepared perfumes, also hung in the air. All groups embraced us and gave words of wisdom. The mothers led by Okosu-ere, after embracing us one by one, wanted to know if we still remembered how our original journey to Erere-ama began. She searched our faces as we answered and seemed reassured by our emphatic, "yes! yes!" She sighed and turned to her fellow mothers.

"Did we not always know in our hearts that these two would come through, triumphant? Yes, we did not doubt. We were confident! Indeed, we knew they had it in them to succeed. We were sure in our hearts that nothing would stop them from winning." They all replied in the affirmative, one after another. She continued.

"Always remember my dear children, that the temptation to use your powers of invincibility just to teach some stupid persons a bitter lesson may sometimes be overwhelming but always turn inward and drink from the nourishing pool of strength and power which lies within you. Whenever you turn inward, Zibobra and all the others who are your constant helpers will be there for you. I know you already know all about this but this little pep talk can only be a source of inspiration for you and a measure of our enduring love for you, my dear children of light." Zibo-ere then knelt down before all the mothers.

"Oh mother Okosu-ere! Oh mothers of light and wisdom. I, Zibo-ere, now do solemnly declare before you all that as we, Layefa and I, depart to fulfill our final mission. We shall carry with us your words of wisdom and your acts of love and we shall do to others and for others what we have gained from you. Our powers will be used at all times for the upliftment of souls and towards the growth of our worlds. We shall maintain the purity of our love as we have through several lifetimes before. We shall always be faithful, Oh Temearau, as we surrender our all to you in us and our fellow beings."

The whole scene was so captivating and so well delivered that it seemed like a well-rehearsed play and I felt like part of an adoring audience. Okosu-ere spread out her arms, palms up.

"Temearau, we the mothers of Erere-ama, being one set of your most loyal and faithful children, do hereby pool our thoughts and unite them with those of Zibo-ere and Layefa for your full and continuing blessings." Her countenance was sober and her voice mellow and strong.

The spectacle and the proclamations brought tears to my eyes. Zibobra gently stepped up to me and wiped away the tears welling up in my eyes.

"Music!" She ordered and soon the soft slow beat of 'kokoma' melody filled the air. Everyone gathered danced gracefully, swaying slowly to the beat. As we danced, lemon colored petals floated in the air above our heads and the tantalizing smells of different perfumes assailed our nostrils. The kokoma music later changed to the fast-paced 'Agene' beats and what hectic dancing this produced! After some time, the Agene beats suddenly changed to the famous 'Owigiri' music and everybody really did some 'wigiring!' Owigiri dance basically involves frenzied gyrations of the body, especially the buttocks, to the fast-paced tempo of the tune. We danced until we felt faint and dizzy. We continued to dance with our eyes closed and I reached out and held Zibo-ere's hand tightly in mine. We continued to dance for a long time and after what seemed like eternity, we opened our eyes realizing with a start, that the music had since stopped.

CHAPTER 8

With this realization came an awareness of the stark reality of the moment. We were inside my car driving homeward at a sedate speed! I was driving and Zibo-ere sat in front beside me and everything appeared normal. However, as we drove along, I began to realize that although it was the same old car I had, everything somehow felt different. It was the same road leading back into town but there were obvious changes all around us. The road, which I remembered to be single lane now had two lanes and traffic was considerably heavier than anticipated. Policemen on the road now appeared in unfamiliar uniform of light-blue instead of the original royal blue. Their looks were menacing and stern and they out-rightly demanded for 'something' when they stopped us, their unfriendly looks belying the plea in their voices.

"We ensure that our roads are safe for both motorists and pedestrians and without us you could not drive so freely." They told us. I checked the dashboard and noted that it was just six in the evening.

"But officer, it is early evening but that aside, I suppose you are being paid for your job? Are you not government employees?" Zibo-ere asked. The policemen looked at us as with pity and shook their heads.

"Madam, you must be a total stranger in this country. Maybe you've been away in some far away oyibo country like America or England or Japan, otherwise, you should have known that the country's police force is the least paid in the whole wide world. We earn proper 'suffer man' salary! Before the second week of the month, your salary is gone and you call that salary? It is almost like working free of charge for the government so the only way we can survive is through 'contributions' from people like you." He concluded, looking at us hopefully.

Zibo-ere realized that the only way we could rid ourselves of the uniformed 'beggars' was to actually give them 'something.' She retrieved her purse from the glove compartment, opened it and gave the man some money. He was effusive in his thanks as the money was shipped out of sight like lightening. As we drove off, we could not help but speculate about the future of our dear country.

The streets looked wider and more beautiful but the people walking at the side of the road and there were a lot of them, wore harassed and agitated looks. Even the few little children we saw looked tough and hardened, having obviously lost their innocence. What a waste! What a pity! How was it possible for things to drastically change for the worse instead of better? Zibo-ere remarked that we may have actually been away for close to thirty years as indicated by the date displayed on the clock in front of the Coca-Cola building we just passed! This awareness sent a chill down my spine. Earth times or periods are surely strange. It definitely did not feel like we had been away for one week, let alone years! Incredible! Absolutely weird!

I could not even remember sleeping a lot at Erere-ama. Could it be that in the finer realms, time stands still or is an illusion? Hmmmm! If we really had been away for that long, then a lot of changes must have taken place not only in the country but in our families as well. Our relatives and friends would have declared us dead long ago and some of them would surely be dead too. We wondered if our parents were still alive and hoped they were. What about Bilflow, Zibo-ere's husband, will he be alive or dead or would he have gone back home to his home country, Denmark? Would he have remarried or could he still be around, waiting for his wife? There were understandably many questions swirling around my mind as we drove through changed but still recognizable streets.

Apart from the major highways, only little physical changes had taken place in the inner city. Here and there, a few new large and colorful buildings could be seen along some streets and two or three posh hotels were particularly outstanding. The changes notwithstanding, we could still identify the old streets and find our way around. We both agreed that the obvious place to go to first was Zibo-ere's house. Soon, we were on the main road leading to their neighborhood. As we drove on, she soberly remarked that her daughter Ebiere, would be a full-grown woman, possibly married with children and that would make her a grandmother.

"But since I still look exactly twenty-seven, the age I was before our shall we say, rediscovery of each other, how will they react? I will no doubt look younger than my daughter! Her child, if she has one, will be very confused. The same thing applies to you too….."

I cut in and quickly reassured her that she had little to worry about on that score. Her charm and radiant love would make all the difference and everybody, including a possible son-in-law, would be enthralled by her personality.

"It is your husband Bilflow that may actually surprise you. He must be quite old now and you know white people age faster than us!"

"Bill will be elderly no doubt but I think he will age well since he has a good stature. I'm sure he will be a distinguished-looking gray haired man, as befits an elder statesman. I do not think I will be too surprised." Zibo-ere said with quiet determination.

I smiled, admiring her courage but actually expecting nothing less of her really. She was the kind of woman who would face any situation with equanimity. She had a resolve that was admirable. All this notwithstanding, there was always a nagging worry about us at the back of my mind. It would be foolish to assume that our bodies, Zibo-ere's and mine, would remain suspended indefinitely in time, as it were. Unless we kept to our vows, it would be difficult for us not to age rapidly. Zibo-ere turned and looked sideways at me. She seemed to have read my thoughts.

"With great love and peace constantly radiating from us, it is not possible to be corrupted by the filth and iniquities in life. Our transition to a higher realm is also in our minds. With this enormous responsibility and the constant reminder in the appearances of our relatives, friends and neighbors about how fast the body and mind ages, we shall be constantly on guard. Yes dear Layefa, we shall remain more or less the way we look until we leave this earth plane. It is a life we freely chose and we shall live it to the fullest. In us shall be found examples of steadfastness, courage, humility, determination, love, discipline, spirituality and other good attributes the human body and soul crave for all the time. Those who come to know or hear about us later will be motivated to emulate us for the betterment of the world. A good number of them will also make our kind of commitment perhaps and achieve their goals. Enough talk for now, dear. Let us go home and meet our families."

On this bright note, we turned off the main road unto an ancillary road. After driving for about one mile, we found ourselves in front of Zibo-ere's house. Amazingly, the gate was exactly the way it was when we left. It never occurred to us to wonder again if Bilflow was dead or had moved and we automatically thought of him as 'old,' since we had been away for so long. More so, we were not too worried about how he would react to our reappearance. Granted he may expect us to look our chronological ages if and when we did reappear but there was nothing either in the way Zibo-ere and I realigned our lives or in the manner we took leave of him that would give him any clue or hope of our ever re-appearing again. I stopped in front of the gate and honked the car horn. After a while, a maiguard opened the gate just a crack, poked his head out and looked at us. He did not look exactly friendly.

"You wan see ma master?" He asked.

"Yes!" We responded.

"Make you holam small, I go see oga and tell am fes."

He then disappeared back into the compound. A minute or so later, his head reappeared.

"Oga say wetin ya name?"

In his haste, he had forgotten to ask our names the first time he came out and we were amused and not at all surprised that his master sent him back to get the identities of the callers. We were later to understand and appreciate the need for the extra caution. Anyhow, we told him our names and he disappeared again. Shortly thereafter, there was commotion inside the compound. We heard a loud exclamation from an unmistakably male Caucasian voice that sounded like Bilflow's. It was repeated again and we could hear more clearly now because I had switched off the car engine.

"Holy Moses! What the….. Goodness gracious! What is this you tell me, Musa? Come and show me! Are you sure you heard them right? You hear them well so, ehn? Musa, tell me. Come here man, let's go and see them!" The voice said in a torrent of excitement.

Next moment, the gate jerked open and a distinguished-looking gray-haired elderly white man stood there looking at us. Since the premises was well lit, we could clearly see him and he could see us too. He made no move to come closer. He just stood there and stared at us in utter shock and bewilderment. Behind him were the maiguard, two young men, a middle-aged man and an elderly woman. Everybody stood where they were and stared at us. We slowly got out of the car and took in the scene before us. Then, with measured and deliberate steps, Zibo-ere walked towards the gate and I followed closely behind her. The elderly white man before us was obviously Zibo-ere's husband, good old Bilflow who had indeed aged gracefully. We stopped when we were within touching distance of him.

"Oh my word! Oh m..myyy word! It's her!" He said in a whisper that was barely audible.

"Na ghost bi dis, abi na the madam true, true?" Someone behind Bilflow asked in a whisper.

"Eei Temearau! Oyinma do-o-eh!" The elderly woman behind Bilflow sobbed gently.

At this point, Zibo-ere stepped forward and enfolded Bilflow in a tight embrace.

"My darling Bill!" With tears of joy running down her cheeks she said, "It's really me, Zibo-ere. It is really me, your wife!" She laughed through her tears.

"Look at me, my dear. Touch me!" she invited, taking both his hands in hers and squeezing them tightly. He looked into her face, dazzled by her youthful beauty and radiance. He was so overcome with emotion that he could only gape at her and stutter.

"Oh no…noo! It can't …be.. It's not …" He mumbled and collapsed in a faint. The young men and the maiguard quickly rushed to him and carried him inside. Zibo-ere turned to the old woman who I later learnt was her mother and embraced her in a tight hug, gently rocking back and forth.

"Nene! Eh Nene!. Okoide Nene! Eh Nene!" Zibo-ere cooed gently. She then turned to me.

"Let us go inside and see how Bill is doing." "In a minute! Let me park the car properly inside the compound first."

I turned and made for the car only to be confronted by a large crowd of curious people that had gathered at the half-opened gate around the car.

Unknown to us, neighbors and passers-by had heard the commotion inside the compound and had come to inquire what the matter was. I gathered later that the Bilflow household was known to be a quiet one and well liked in the neighborhood. He rarely received visitors except for his old mother-in-law who came and stayed with him from time to time and one or two of his relatives from his home country. Though occasionally, a few in-laws also visited. On the whole, he was known to be the quiet sort who minded his own business. So it was understandable that neighbors became curious and a little concerned when unusual noises were heard within the compound. As I made my way towards the car, I heard snippets of conversations all around me. Some said the gardener told them that Bilflow's long lost wife had returned. The story sounded incredible and unbelievable since many had presumed her dead long, long ago.

"How can one explain a situation where one's wife just goes off without leaving a contact address and never contacted anyone, ever? She was never ever seen by any living soul for an extremely long period. Can you imagine that?" One old man in the crowd asked rhetorically.

"How can any responsible woman leave her husband for a long, long time without a word? What stupid nonsense! Aaboo! Man na wood? Let the man beware-O! Who knows where she has been since!" Another added in righteous indignation.

Most of the people were of the opinion that it was because the woman was married to a white man that she could do such an outrageous thing and get away with it.

"You cannot be married to a hot-blooded African and think that you, the wife, can come and go whenever and however you please! It is because she is married to a white man." They contended.

I finally succeeded in squeezing into the car, started it and drove into the compound. The maiguard locked the gate after me with some difficulty because of the crowd outside.

"Wonders, oh wonders... This is America wonder!" I heard a woman say before I walked inside, out of earshot.

The scene inside was not too different from the one outside. The difference was only in numbers. There were fewer people inside. Happily, Bilflow had recovered and everyone was talking at once. All present wanted to touch Zibo-ere and ask her questions.

It was sheer bedlam and no one seemed to pay the least attention to me. I made my way to the well-stocked bar, avoiding the excited crowd in the center of the living room and made myself a large drink of Campari on the rocks. I sat on one of the bar stools and contemplated the situation at hand. I thought of breaking up the conversations going on simultaneously in the living room among Zibo-ere, her mother, Bilflow and the others but decided against it. Bilflow was bound to redirect the gathering sooner or later so he could have some private talk with his wife, I reasoned. My glass was soon empty so I refilled it and tried to catch Ziboere's attention by looking over people's shoulders and between heads but I could not so I just relaxed. Not long after, Bilflow extricated himself from the group and came over to the bar, calling out my name happily. I stood up and took his extended hand in a firm handshake before encasing him in a bear hug. He was emotional and could not speak but just held me tightly for a long time before releasing me.

"My dear fellow," he began.

"How can I ever thank you enough for bringing Zib back to me. Frankly Layefa, words cannot describe how I feel. My happiness knows no bounds and I am sincerely grateful to you."

I patted him on the shoulder and told him that I perfectly understood how he felt.

"There is really no need to thank me, my dear Bill. I did what was expected of me. For what you are to Zibo-ere, you don't need to thank me Bill. You are a treasure." We both sat down again on the stools at the bar.

"Oh!" He said, standing up again. I stood up with him.

"The joy of the moment has made me forget my manners. Please forgive me."

Clapping his hands for attention, he moved towards the group surrounding Zibo-ere and announced in a loud voice that everyone should have a drink to celebrate the occasion. He then ordered the cook to prepare dinner for everyone. It was already late in the evening and he was sure we were hungry. He also gave instructions for the guest room to be prepared for me.

After sitting me down firmly in one of the sofas, he dashed back to the bar and prepared drinks for everyone. Lemon and orange juice for Zibo-ere and her mother, Campari on the rocks for me. He was all over the place, dishing out instructions here and there while Zibo-ere watched him fondly.

CHAPTER 9

*E*ven though it was quite late in the night, the phone in the house began to ring almost non-stop as friends and close associates who had heard about Zibo-ere's home-coming called to confirm and congratulate the family. How the news had traveled at lightning speed was a mystery. Dinner was eventually ready and Bilflow insisted that everyone, including the house helps eat at the same table. This gesture seemed to delight Zibo-ere as she embraced him lovingly.

"Oh my darling Bill!" She exclaimed, beaming radiantly.

Dinner was a very lively affair. Everybody chatted and joked and laughed freely without inhibition. Let's face it, how often does a spouse disappear without a single trace for as long as thirty years and then suddenly reappear looking even younger and more beautiful? Not very often, you must agree. In fact, not ever! Not even the Guinness Book of World Records could boast of such a record. It therefore qualified as a momentous occasion. Yes, it was indeed memorable and no one could blame Bilflow for going just a little overboard. As a matter of fact, it would have been strange if he had not reacted the way he did, considering the deep affection he had for Zibo-ere before their unexpected separation. We talked excitedly through dinner while King Robert Ebizimor's popular 'wiri hun-hun!' record played in the background. After the meal, we all retired to the living room while the household staff went about their duties. It was unlikely that anyone would sleep.

Our discussions in the living room were more like a question and answer session. Everyone asked Zibo-ere and me questions. Bilflow had telephoned their daughter Ebiere, now married and living with her husband Oyinpreye, in the United States of America. He placed the call immediately he confirmed that the person in front of him was indeed, Zibo-ere.

Ebiere already had a set of twins, a boy and a girl, aged ten. Expectedly, she had been wild with excitement Bilflow said and had promised that the entire family would fly over as soon as the secure seats on the next available flight to see their lost but now found mother and grandmother. Zibo-ere too was anxious to see her daughter again and get acquainted with her son-in-law and grandchildren. Everything was as she and I had speculated on our return when we realized that we had actually been away from our earthly homes for a very long time. Bilflow reminded the cook to prepare a banquet the following evening when, all things being equal, Ebiere and her family would have arrived. All other persons at dinner were persuaded to go to bed and we pressed Zibo-ere's mother to do likewise. She reluctantly agreed after originally insisting that she was not tired at all. It was obvious she wanted to spend more time, if not the whole night, with her daughter. She profusely thanked Temearau for giving her the opportunity of seeing her beloved daughter once again before calling her away to her final home. Bidding her daughter goodnight, she embraced her affectionately in our traditional atuu fashion chest-to-chest and cheek-to-cheek.

"I can now die happy, Oh Temearau! I can now die peacefully."

She said, tears of joy glistening in her eyes as she stood up to leave.

She bid the rest of us goodnight and made her dignified exit, accompanied by Ziboere.

"Hmm!" Bilflow sighed deeply.

"What a dear, dear mother, Nene! She has been a pillar of strength and has come to mean a lot to me." He said theatrically.

There was a period of brief silence as everybody seemed to be lost in his or her own private thoughts. Though not tired at all, I felt the need to retire for the night, if one could call past four in the morning 'night' that is! Husband and wife needed to re-bond I reasoned but before this suggestion could be made, Bilflow broke the silence.

"Well, well, well, my dear fellow! What can I say? How can I begin?"

He seemed to be truly short of words to express himself and that was a surprise for a man like him, known for his eloquence. Zibo-ere was sitting close to him on the sofa and he put his arm around her and drew her close.

"But tell me Layefa," he continued, "how is it that my darling is still looking this young and beautiful? And you too come to think of it, even though I knew you for only a day. It is as if time stood still for both of you."

"My dear Bill, all will become clear when Zibo-ere explains our mission fully to you. You will understand why we are still this way when you realize that we have reached the point of being in complete harmony with our world. I will leave the explaining to Zibo-ere. Meanwhile, let me take leave of you at this time. It is already quite late. Goodnight old fellow! Sleep well."

I stood up and took his hand in a firm handshake. I also bid Zibo-ere goodnight and made my way to the guest room. In as much as Zibo-ere and I were soul mates, she still needed her husband in the real world. It was therefore prudent to leave them alone. The beautiful thing about the relationship between us was its total selflessness. We were prepared at any time to make any kind of sacrifice for each other, no matter how great. By maintaining the sanctity of our spiritual love, we ensured its longevity. No doubt, in the course of the night, Zibo-ere will explain all we had passed through during our sojourn in the higher realms to her husband. All manner of thoughts whirled through my mind as I went to the guest room. I changed into a pair of pajamas provided by Bilflow and got into bed. I must have slept off the minute my head touched the pillow. In no at all, I was in dream land, walking down what appeared to be a country road. It was late afternoon and the sun was beginning to set. There was heavy pedestrian traffic on both sides. I was taking a leisurely stroll and was soon surrounded by six beautiful girls who jostled amongst themselves for my attention. They sent suggestive messages through their body languages. I pointedly ignored them and just kept on walking. Before I realized what was happening, I had been whisked off my feet by these same girls! They carried me shoulder-high down the road singing merrily. After a while, we came to a clear blue river, obviously the destination of my bearers. It was quieter here and there was no one else around except the girls and me. Giggling, they stripped off my clothes down to my underpants and threw me into the river.

They then dived in and swarm around me, beating the water with their hands, laughing and thoroughly enjoying themselves. I must have also enjoyed the swim because I do not remember having any unpleasant or queasy feeling while in their company. In a swift change of scene, I found myself being driven in a shiny new car. I was in the back seat and soon realized I was not alone. I turned sideways to get a better look at my companion and found myself staring into the dark brown eyes of a very beautiful girl sitting demurely by me. She was one of the young ladies that bathed with me at the river a while back. A close relationship was established right there and then as I engaged her in conversation. In no time at all, we were making marriage plans! Next thing I knew, I was journeying to a beautiful far-away country aboard an airplane. The plane was crowded and everybody was feeling happy and excited. It was like a party in the sky and we had a hilarious time.

As is typical with dreams, from the plane I found myself in a worship environment. I was in a large cathedral. Everywhere was absolutely quiet and serene. I was so deep in meditation that I did not notice other people present. Then, faint noises pierced my consciousness. It was the sound of distant church bells, sounding very far off at first but gradually growing louder and louder. I was rudely woken by a knock on the bedroom door.

I sat up and rubbed my eyes while trying to remember where I was. The person knocked a second time.

"Oga, are you awake? A voice from behind the door inquired. "Yes, please come in."

The steward entered and apologized for waking me up but he wanted to know if I would need warm water for my bath.

"The water heater is not working at the moment so if you want hot water, I will have to heat some for you," he said.

I thanked him for his thoughtfulness but told him that cold water would do just fine.

"Oga and madam want you to join them for breakfast," he informed me and left, shutting the door gently behind him.

Still lying in bed, I tried to arrange my plans for the day. I decided that I must leave after breakfast. I had to look for my old friend and neighbor, Keme-owei. I wondered if he was still at the flat close to mine.

Whatever be the case, I must find him because I intended to get as much information as possible about what became of my apartment after I left as well as my parents reaction to my disappearance. I tried to imagine how he would look now and the expression on his face when he sees me. The thought of his reaction brought a smile to my lips. It must have been a shock for him and all my relatives and friends when they realized that I had vanished from the face of the earth, just like that!

Like many families whose loved ones disappeared into the hands of ritual killers and head hunters, my friends and family would have thrown up their hands helplessly. They would have just prayed that 'God should help' so that Layefa too does not become a statistical dot, one of the numerous citizens to be so counted. By now, everyone must have given up all hope of ever seeing me again. Quite understandable all must agree. I could not help but speculate about Keme-owei. Would he have improved materially, with a big house and a chain of cars and a large staff? Well, O'l boy, you can put your flights of fancy and speculations to rest as you will find out for soon enough, I told myself.

All the while, I had somehow not allowed thoughts of my parents dwell on my mind. But inevitably my heart turned to them. I thought of my dear mother and tried to imagine the emotional torture she must have endured while waiting hopefully for my return. Did she eventually resign to fate when it became obvious that I was not likely to come back? My mother was extremely fond of me so must have been grief-stricken beyond words. She was a very optimistic person and must have still hoped, no matter how slim the hope was, that I was alive.

Numerous cases of missing persons who remained unaccounted for forever would not have helped matters though. My heart ached for her.

Then, I thought of my father. Before I left, Papa had newly acquired a passion for Christianity, having become 'born-again.' I imagined how he must have copiously quoted from the Bible in his bid to console my mother by putting up a facade of total resignation to the will of God. Notwithstanding the front, deep in his heart, he must have grieved too. My father had always seen in me a bright and shiny star, someone he was convinced would one day become a leader of great repute in our community. My sudden and inexplicable disappearance would have been a big blow, shattering his tall dreams for me, though he would have given the impression of unruffled calmness. I prayed that he had received divine revelation that I was still alive and alright. Such insight would have given him enough strength and fortitude to cushion the whole family. As time went on however, my long sojourn must have caused hope to wane especially amongst the less optimistic. I could not wait to see the expression on his face when he sets his eyes on me. I took a leisurely bath with these nostalgic thoughts of family and friends running through my mind.

Afterwards, I dressed in some casual clothes provided by Bilflow, then left the room to join them in the dining room for breakfast. I pondered what had happened to us in such a short time. Was it really correct to say that all that happened to Zibo-ere and I, took place within a short space of time? To our relatives and friends, it must have been a life time of anxiety and even despair but to us, it was no more than a couple of days. Yes, days! I thanked the Almighty again for the opportunity granted me to have this fantastic experience.

CHAPTER 10

Bilflow hailed me as I reached the dining room. He looked much younger and full of smiles as he approached and gave me a hearty handshake.

"I trust you slept well?" He inquired, smiling broadly. I told him I did and complimented him on his fresh looks.

"Yes, I feel so much lighter. In fact, I feel ten years younger, as if a reinvigorating spirit had been pumped into my veins!" He joked.

"I'm so happy for you, Bill. I am sure you deserve every happiness and good fortune that fate brings your way. When will Ziboere join us?" I asked after a while. He told me that she was with her mother and would join us shortly.

"We decided that the old woman should have her breakfast in bed and Zib wanted to serve her personally," he replied.

"In that case, please allow me pay my respects to her mother." I requested.

"By all means!" He responded, leading the way out of the dining room to his mother-in-law's room.

As we approached the room, he gently caught me by the arm and confided that the old woman had not been feeling too well for some time now and he did not think she had much longer to live. He said the unusual tranquility of her countenance this morning gave him course for worry. It was as though she had already made up her mind and was now ready for the next phase of existence. She was truly grateful that Temearau answered her prayers by giving her the opportunity of seeing her beloved daughter once again. I halted in my tracks and stared at him in surprise but he pulled me gently by the hand. If this was so Zibo-ere, with her perceptiveness must have sensed something. Little wonder then that she was spending much time with her mother as it may perhaps be her last moments with her.

We soon got to the door leading to the room and Bilflow knocked softly and entered without waiting for an answer. I followed closely behind. We both came to a standstill, transfixed with mouths agape as we took in the pathetic scene before us. Bilflow's intuition had been right after all. Zibo-ere sat at the edge of the bed cradling the head of her mother, rocking her gently. She looked up at us as we entered, tears streaming down her cheeks. Bilflow was immediately by her side and put his arms around her. Then, he gently removed the dead woman from her arms and laid her out on the bed.

"There is nothing you or anyone else can do for her now, darling. She's with her maker now and thankfully, you had the opportunity of not only seeing her alive but biding her farewell." He told her softly.

"Let's call the doctor and arrange to take her to the mortuary. At least, she died a happy woman as you can see from her countenance."

Ziboere just sat still, staring into space oblivious of what he had said.

"Come now my dear," he urged, taking her hands.

As she got up, she turned and stared at me. I reached for her hand involuntarily and held it reassuringly.

"You should be glad that she transited, a happy woman.

Temearau gave her the grace to see and hold you before the final call. Look, she's smiling down radiantly at us!" I told her staring up at the ceiling. Zibo-ere sobbed as she was led away from the bed.

"Oh, Mother! Mother!" She stopped at the door and gave the corpse a last look.

"Until we meet again dearest mother, enjoy your deserved rest. Baiyo! Baiyo!"

Then she broke down again and wept as Bilflow led her out of the room. Already close to tears myself, I stood alone in the room for a while and observed the corpse. Then, wishing her a joyous passage, I slowly walked out, closing the door gently behind me. As news of Opu Nene's demise spread through the house, there was sadness because everyone was very fond of her. Breakfast was forgotten and we all sat in the living room mourning. Zibo-ere just sat in one of the sofas and stared blankly into space, emitting sighs and sobs every now and then.

The sudden transition of Zibo-ere's mother brought about a change in my plans. I decided to postpone my departure by one more day, thinking it proper that I tarry awhile and render whatever assistance I could to my soul-mate and her family. From morning until late in the afternoon, Bilflow was in and out of the house making arrangements for a quick burial. I accompanied him to a number of places, including the homes of close relatives of the deceased. It was decided that she be taken to her village, Ebiama, for a befitting funeral. The belief in her family was that the departed soul would not enter its rightful abode if buried in a foreign place.

"Besides," they told us, "no true Izon person ever allowed his or her bones to rest in a distant land. Those who fail to have the bones properly interred always suffered for It."

Bilflow was not a stranger to the customs and traditions of the Izons and he readily agreed. Arrangements were soon in top gear for the conveyance of the body, which had since been taken to the mortuary, to Ebiama for burial rites and interment.

We finally got home in the evening to meet another surprise, this time, a pleasant one. Ebiere and her family had arrived from the United States of America! Ebiere, Zibo-ere's daughter, was barely five years old when her mother and I went off to Erere-ama. She had turned out to become a stunning beauty. Accompanied by the twins and her husband Oyinpreye, the family had caught the first available flight out of their base. On reaching Eselemo, they beheld a mother that had been lost for so long. A grandmother that had never been seen by the twins and mother-in-law that was yet to be known by her son in-law. Everything however turned out to be an anti-climax of sorts as what should have been a happy re-union was marred by the somber and mournful mood in the house, occasioned by the sudden passing of Opu Nene. We must have come in soon after their arrival as we met them in the living room where Zibo-ere had remained since morning. Ebiere, who was sitting between Zibo-ere and Oyinpreye stood up and ran to her father as soon as we entered the room.

"Daddy!" She called, arms outstretched.

Bilflow enfolded her in a tight embrace and for a few moments they just stood there comforted in each other's arms. I knew it was Ebiere the moment I saw her. She was almost an exact replica of her mother. The only differences were Ebiere's complexion and shoulder length reddish-brown hair. Her husband Oyinpreye was also biracial with an American mother and African father. He was slim, tall, handsome and appeared to have a pleasant disposition.

The twins had same complexion as their mother but had black hair. They were lively, vivacious and all over the place, trying to satisfy their curious minds. It appeared this was their first visit to the country. However, the gloomy mood in the house was infectious and soon got to them as they looked from face to face, trying to determine what the matter was. Ebiere soon disengaged herself from her father and went over to Zibo-ere, who was now standing by a window. The meeting between mother and daughter was as touching as it was emotional. Ebiere held her mother tight and could not say a word for a long time. Tears flowed down her face and fell on her mother's blouse. Zibo-ere just held her, cooing words of endearment.

"Oh baby, my baby! My little angel!" She repeated over and over as her eyes also filled with tears. Bilflow went over and led them to a settee. He was barely holding back tears I noticed. It was such a moving scene. The death of Zibo-ere's mother made it all the more somber. I moved uneasily around, really quite uncomfortable in the tearful setting before me. Oyinpreye, together with the twins went over to sit with his wife and parents in-law and it was soon one big family embrace. I went over to the bar, fixed myself a drink and sat on one of the bar stools then discretely turned my back and wiped a tear or two from my eyes.

They broke up shortly after and Zibo-ere gave Oyinpreye a tight hug, telling him how delighted she was to meet 'my dear son,' as she called him. He told her he too was very pleased to finally meet her as he had been looking forward to this moment for a long time. It was obvious that they immediately took to each other and Ebiere was particularly happy about this. She then turned her attention to the twins, kissing and fussing over them. Everyone was soon laughing excitedly and the gloom in the house momentarily lightened. Ebiere came over to where I was sitting and hugged me. Oyinpreye and the twins also came over and shook hands with me politely. Zibo-ere had already named the twins Bolou-ere, for the girl and Ebi-owei, for the boy.

"It's so good to see you again, little angel!" I said.

The children giggled in amusement as they heard their mother being referred to as 'little angel.'

Understandingly, they were curious and looked from one face to the other. Bilflow summoned the house keeper and gave instructions for them to be bathed, fed and made comfortable. The instruction was promptly obeyed and the twins were taken away. Bilflow briefed everyone about the arrangements being made for the burial of Opu Nene as soon as possible, as was her wish. Ebiere and Oyinpreye both expressed sadness and were particularly pained that they missed seeing her again by just a few hours.

"If we had come yesterday we would probably have met her alive," Oyinpreye said despairingly.

"My dear old Opu Nene! I wish I could have said goodbye," Ebiere lamented.

"Oh mama, were you with her when she passed? Did she talk to you?" She asked, turning to look at her mother.

"Yes, indeed, I was with her and we talked until her last breath. She sent you her special love my dear and hoped that you'd be around for the funeral."

"How was she mama? Was she happy, sad or what?"

Ebiere wanted to know.

"Oh she was quite happy. You can rest assured that she died a happy woman, especially after seeing me again."

Oyinpreye moved closer to Zibo-ere and took her hand in his.

"I am glad that Opu Nene saw you again mama. She always talked about you, we were told and it would have been very sad if she had died unfulfilled. For this mama, we should be very grateful. May her gentle soul find companionship among the angels!" He prayed.

"Well, why don't you all clean up and rest for a while before dinner. You have hardly rested since you arrived."

"But Daddy!" Ebiere protested.

"Nobody has told us about mama's experience. I am dying of curiosity and I'm sure Preye is too. We've waited too long for this moment and nobody's going to tell us to wait any longer. So mama, there is no way we can eat or bathe or do anything until we have heard all that you have to tell us," she said with a note of finality.

It was obvious Zibo-ere was not ready to delve into the story yet. Seeing her reluctance, I tactically took sides with Bilflow and urged them to relax for a while and give Zibo-ere some time to rest too.

"It is not a story you hear in a hurry my dear," I told Ebiere.

"Especially Oyinpreye who must be quite confused about it all. We have to consider your kids as well. They must be just as curious about their long lost grandmother who still looks so young and beautiful! I think it is proper that they be present too when the story is told."

"But uncle Layefa, I'm all keyed up to learn what happened to mama all these years! I am too excited and impatient and happy and...."

"Hey! Hey! Easy! Take it easy!" I protested raising my arms in mock horror. Everyone laughed and the undercurrent of tension, which had threatened to surface, melted away. I wondered if Ebiere still remembered me or it was out of mere courtesy that she called me uncle. She was only five years old when we disappeared, too young then to understand what was happening. Zibo-ere called her daughter and held her close, kissing her on the forehead as she must have done countless times when Ebiere was a child.

"Darling, it is my greatest desire to tell you what happened to me during your growing up years and why I was not around. Please know that at every moment, even though I wasn't with you physically, I was always with you spiritually though you may not have been aware of it. For now, I still think your daddy's right. It would be better for you all to rest a little and freshen up. Thereafter I promise, I will tell you everything."

She immediately got up after this little speech and Ebiere and Oyinpreye did likewise. Then she gently steered them in the direction of their bedroom. They reluctantly went out leaving the three of us behind.

It did not take long for neighbors, friends and relations to start dropping by to sympathize with the family on the death of Ziboere's mother and also to rejoice with Bilflow on the homecoming of his wife. It was a mixed feeling of sadness and joy but the air of celebration seemed to carry the day especially with the added arrival of Ebiere and her family. Everyone generally agreed that Opu Nene died a good death since she was quite old and also had the pleasure of seeing her beloved daughter again. The house was a beehive of activities until late in the night and even Ebiere and Preye had to come back to the living room to be greeted by some of the visitors. At last, the last caller left and we were once again alone in the sitting room. I then informed Zibo-ere and Bilflow about my intention to postpone my planned trip.

"It is only natural for me to be eager to go home and see my family but considering the latest developments around here, I feel my presence will be of some use. However, the postponement can only be for a day as I must leave for home the day after tomorrow. I shall of course come back for Opu Nene's funeral when the date is fixed." Bilflow thanked me for being considerate while Zibo-ere just took my hand, squeezed it and smiled gratefully.

"It is selfish of me I know but I'd hoped that you would stay until after my mother's funeral. There's no gainsaying the fact that I could also use your support in explaining our experiences to Ebiere, her husband and children. Moreover, you are an integral part of my story so your presence would help a lot. I thank you for deferring your trip for another day. Though I would have liked you to stay a bit longer, I realize you must also visit your family so they will know you are still alive and well."

"You are not being selfish at all," I assured her. "After all we've been through together and now know about each other, it is only natural for you to feel such sentiments. Destiny has brought us together and I am sure our families will be all the better for it…"

"I'm quite moved by all this talk old chap," Bilflow cut in. He had been quiet all this while.

"I consider it a privilege to share in my own way, the experiences you and my darling have been through."

He put his arm around Zibo-ere possessively. When your story gets told many years from now, it may sound incredible to some. A lot of people will not only find it unbelievable but consider it an old folklore or fairytale. Only a few discerning ones enlightened by years of deep reflection, will read between the lines and get the import of the story. Then those of us who had had the privilege of knowing you, will be considered lucky and envied. Once again, I thank you for your understanding." He paused dramatically and looked at me.

"You know I'll always consider you a member of our family from now on because of Zib who has turned out to be your soulmate. I pray that your return brings the same joy and happiness to your family that our family now enjoys and will continue to enjoy until the end of our days."

He touched me lightly on the shoulder then turned and kissed his wife affectionately on her forehead.

"Thank you sweetheart!" Zibo-ere said, smiling at him fondly.

"It's already late and we must all get ourselves ready for dinner. Remember that the cook is preparing a rare delicacy to celebrate the joy of the moment so we should all get our appetites sharp and ready. I think you could use some freshening up," she said to me.

"Bill and I could do with some too. We'll disperse now and reassemble in say, an hour's time…" she suggested.

We all agreed and I slowly made my way to the guest room. While in the shower, an old favorite song of mine titled, 'You're Never Alone' came to mind and I hummed it softly. The song particularly mirrored my thoughts and soon I began to sing it out in a low tone.

You may think you're alone most times
But let me tell you
You're surrounded all the time
Surrounded on all sides
By unseen beings
Who are attracted to you
And do your bidding
So be careful my friend.
They have neither friend nor foe
They will swarm around you
Helping you as you desire
But neither as friend nor foe
So don't ever be fooled
By what they say sometimes.
Have you any control
Over circumstances?
Who can change destiny they ask
So always remember
That you're never alone
But friend, thoughts attract
Intense thoughts that occupy us materialize
Such thoughts, my friend
Are products of unseen energies
Which surround you on all sides
Awaiting your pleasure
So remember always my friend
To help fulfill your destiny
For you're never alone.
You're surrounded by unseen beings and energies
Eager to do your bidding
So bid cautiously, bid carefully
Because you're never alone.

The song made me reflect on life. What lessons can be learnt from this good old song? Human beings have a way of running away from their responsibilities, especially difficult ones. We try to dodge and shift the burden or find some explanations. What better excuse can there be than that your fate in life has been predestined? You readily agree with the school of thought that we are really not responsible for how our lives turn out. It is all a function of one's destiny they say.

You believe everything is pre-ordained and there is hardly anything one can do to change one's assigned lot in life. But the opposite school of thought that believes in the role of volition and freewill forces us to be accountable for all our actions. Chance does not come in at all and we are expected to play an active role in the processes that lead to the actualization of our destiny. In other words, we are responsible for our destiny in life. Everything we do consciously and unconsciously, either as a result of knowledge or ignorance, affects the outcome of our destiny and we should be held accountable. Put another way, we should hold ourselves accountable for where we are in life.

The second school of thought contends that we cannot go committing all sorts of crimes and when we are called to answer for them, give all manner of excuses. This type of criminal will not be man enough to accept his responsibilities but will be bold enough to even kill for money or whatever.

Take this experience that Zibo-ere and I have just had. Can one rightly say it was preordained that we would begin the experience at precisely the time we did? Another would aver that we both worked through several lifetimes for the privilege of this culminating act and as such, it could not have been predestined. Volition was at play here, though mostly in the subconscious. What about the special grace of the Creator? Can there be such special grace without seemingly any effort on our part?

CHAPTER 11

I was still turning these questions over in my mind when a knock on the door reminded me of dinner.

"I'll be out in a second!" I called out and quickly dressed up. Everyone had assembled for pre-dinner drinks by the time I entered the living room. Oyinpreye was behind the bar serving drinks. The twins wore colorful jean suits embroidered with Mickey Mouse figures. They sat between their grandparents, Bilflow and Zibo-ere and it was apparent that they were bombarding them with questions. It was a happy family setting and Ebiere could not hide her joy as she laughed at some of the questions.

It soon became obvious to all that no meaningful discussion could take place with the twins around. They were determined to be the center of attention and everybody had to be patient and tolerant with them. We finished our drinks and moved over to the dining table for the celebration dinner earlier announced. We lingered over dinner which was indeed quite delicious and everyone had their fill.

Efforts to send the twins off to bed after dinner were of no avail as they stoutly refused to go, although barely awake. Inevitably, dear friend sleep overtook them and they were carried off to bed at about eleven o'clock. We adults could now have some serious discussions as we settled down with cups of tea. Zibo-ere had just started to tell the story when we heard a loud noise outside. Someone was shouting and banging on the front door as if his life depended on it. "Open up Mr. Forest!

Open up!"

We all looked wildly at ourselves then Bilflow got up and strode to the front door. We rushed after him.

"Who are you?" He shouted.

Without waiting for an answer, he threw the door open and we were confronted by a small crowd of about ten persons. The maiguard had been overpowered and trussed up like a Christmas turkey in a corner of the compound. The man who had been knocking on the door, obviously their leader, held a big stick in his right hand and a cock in his left. He looked fierce and determined, was bare-chested and clad in a wrapper tied around his loins. Some of the other men were similarly clad.

"What is the meaning of this…?" Bilflow began but was cut off by the leader.

"Oyibo, shut your mouth and come out here!" He shouted.

All this while, we were all huddled behind Bilflow, looking out at the crowd before us and standing just inside the door. None of us dared step outside because of the imminent danger we perceived. The noise had woken up the household staff and all of them came out from their rooms and stared through the windows.

"Bilflow, let me go out and meet them," I said, restraining him from stepping outside to confront the people.

"Bill, please let Layefa go and talk to them," Zibo-ere also concurred. Bilflow agreed as he probably also realized that it would be safer for him.

"Okay!" He said and I went outside and faced the people.

"Let the oyibo man come out and face us. We want to see him!" The leader was still insistent and a murmur of agreement swept through the crowd.

"Yes, let the oyibo man come out!" They also insisted, almost chanting.

"Look my friends," I began in a conciliatory tone.

"I am a member of Mr. Forest's family. You can talk to me. Mr. Forest is an old man and the strain of addressing such an intimidating assemblage will not be good for him. I assure you that whatever the problem is can be handled to your satisfaction." The leader considered what I had just said, looked at his people and reluctantly agreed.

"Okay! But let him not move out of our sight," he warned. "We are representatives of the landowners in this community. Many of us know this man Mr. Forest, as a peace-loving man. He minds his own business, that we know. But something unheard of has happened in our village. You see, even though every part of our village is now developed and is called township or city, our traditional enclaves are still villages. Yes, villages within a city. Do you see this cock I'm holding?" He asked, raising the hand that held the cock.

"Yes, I see it." I responded.

"Good! Is it usual for someone to be carrying a cock about like this at this time of the night?"

I replied in the negative, struggling to figure out what the man was up to. Since cocks are usually associated with rituals especially among traditionalists, I thought perhaps that they wanted some donations. What baffled me however, was why they should be so crude about it. No one would be compelled to make donations especially for purposes that they knew nothing about.

"Do you hear?" The leader was asked.

"What? What did you say?" I questioned.

I had missed the point he made. He looked at me a little angrily then went on a long narration about what they heard transpired in Bilflow's house, including the fact that wizardry was used to bring Zibo-ere back from the dead and what all these further portended for the people.

"What!" I shouted, completely nonplussed.

"But… but that cannot be." I stuttered as I looked uncertainly at the people.

I turned around and looked at Bilflow and the others gathered at the front door. They too were stunned. Before I could respond adequately, Zibo-ere stepped outside regally, head held high and stood by me facing the crowd.

"My dear people," she began, the stunned expression now gone.

"You say this oyibo man Mr. Forest, is a wizard who caused his long dead wife that is me, to rise from the dead?"

As she spoke, her features softened and her face took on a serene appearance. A hush fell on the crowd and some of them moved back a little. I remembered that the maiguard was still tied up and went up and untied the poor fellow as Zibo-ere continued talking.

"You say his dead wife who was brought back to life has resulted in the greatest calamity that ever befell your community. One night alone three boys and a girl died. The next night witnessed deaths of the oldest chief, one old woman and a child. This very morning, a speeding motorcycle knocked down and killed an old woman who was crossing the road. You have never before experienced this number of deaths at once in your community, so you have consulted the oracle which prescribed the sacrifice of cocks, goats and other things. According to you, the oracle also said that the oyibo man's wife that is me, must make sacrifices to appease the gods of the land. You further explained with more emphasis that the oyibo man has to pay for all the dead souls and must accompany you to your shrine where the manner of payment will be made known to him."

She paused, hands clasped in front of her and eyes closed as if in prayer. She spread out her arms and everyone held their breath and watched. Suddenly, a young girl burst out of the crowd and ran towards the spot where Zibo-ere stood, screaming shrilly. She did a weird dance, still screaming. After some time, the girl suddenly stopped and fell face down. We all thought she had passed out but she got up again as suddenly as she had fallen. Jumping from side to side, she pointed her finger at Zibo-ere and began to scream.

"I can see them. O! Yes, I can see them!" She wailed. By this time, the crowd which had been growing, had almost tripled. The leader went up to her and tried to make her tell him who it was she saw. But it was to no avail. She was delirious and just went on and on about how they were surrounded.

"Ey, they have surrounded us! We are surrounded O-o! See! See that one over there!" She pointed at nothing in particular.

"See e-e-h! He is coming to catch me e-e! Oh no! No! Please, don't let him touch me!" Then she looked up suddenly.

"Look everyone! There's a cover over you. Look up now!" She said and everyone looked up instinctively.

"What do you see above your heads? Can't you see all those flying beings above you? They are warning us, shaking their fingers at us!"

She sighed and collapsed to the ground again. This time she was truly out. The throng outside was just as confused and bemused by what the girl had said as we were. Nobody could see anything unusual above them. The leader conferred with some other men in the crowd then turned and faced us, keeping his distance.

"Oyibo man's madam, see what has happened to this girl right before us? It is all part of the mystical powers you and your husband must possess. If she too dies, you will pay dearly. What further proof do we need to convince us that you and your husband have magical and evil powers hn?" He asked.

"Look, my friend, " I began, moving towards him. He raised the cock and shook it menacingly at me.

"Stop right there! Don't come near me!" He barked.

"If you come any closer, you will be sorry for yourself."

Of course the ferocity of his expression and the harsh and unfriendly tone stopped me in my tracks and I took a few cautious steps backwards. What a crazy fellow, I thought and sighed inwardly. The situation required delicate handling and I could not say I was doing very well. I had noticed that despite all the threats and intimidation from the crowd, they had shown some reverence for Zibo-ere when she addressed them. I thought perhaps she could handle it better than I was doing. So I tactfully retreated. Not that I was running away from trouble, though! In fact, the change in tactics was all in a bid to solve the problem. I felt that her high sensitivity in human dealings and her natural love for all, qualified her eminently to deal with the situation at hand. As if on cue, she shook her head sadly and addressed the group but looked particularly at the leader.

"My dear friend," she said to him.

"Please put down that cock and the stick you're holding. There's not going to be any fight here so please, put them down."

The man appeared flustered. He looked at Zibo-ere furtively and also glanced at his group as if seeking permission. Zibo-ere continued to look steadily at him, commanding him with her gaze and forcing him to turn his attention to her. Then slowly, he bent down and put the cock and the stick on the ground. The cock's legs were tied and it flapped its wings about for some time before settling down.

"Thank you!" She said, voice soft but audible to everyone. Dramatically, she spread her arms wide, palms up. Everyone's attention now riveted on her. Looking up to the sky she began to speak, first in a low tone, which gradually increased in pitch until it reached a crescendo.

"Ey Temerau! Temearau! look with pity upon your children here gathered. Have mercy on them for they are ignorant and unaware of the implications of their actions. Open their minds to your infinite goodness and beauty. Your beauty abounds everywhere but many fail to see. Oh celestial beings of light, help these humans who may be doomed to pass through life without being affected positively by the vibrant and miraculous gifts that are everywhere in this world."

She stopped for a moment and looked directly at the protesters.

"Oh you people of good heritage that prefer to wallow in the depths of self-imposed filth. Look within yourselves for solutions to your calamities and misfortunes, which will continue unabated until you live up to the realities around you."

An angry murmur swept through the crowd as they heard these last words which were spoken directly to them. The leader, a deep frown on his face, separated himself from the others. He walked to where the girl still lay on the ground unconscious and shook her vigorously until she opened her eyes, groaned and sat up. Satisfied that she was all right and had not died, he turned and faced Ziboere. Standing with hands akimbo and wearing a stern expression, he challenged her to prove their accusations wrong.

"All you have said is talk. Just talk! You have not said anything concrete and we shall not leave until we are satisfied."

The crowd was in agreement with him. A flash of lightening lit up the dark sky just as he finished talking.

"Tufia!" He hissed and so did the entire crowd. Another flash of lightening cut through the air again just as the crowd finished hissing. There is a general belief that evil usually accompanies lightening and that hissing as it flashed would avert the evil, so all in the group dutifully hissed again, looking uncertainly at each other.

As we all looked up at the sky wondering if it was going to rain, there was yet another flash of lightening, this time followed by a loud clap of thunder. It appeared as if it would rain but the sky was unusually clear and many shivered involuntarily. A chill of apprehension went down my spine. Zibo-ere called to Bilflow to join her outside. Even though the night was far spent, everyone was still alert and none appeared the least bit fatigued.

"Bilflow dear, come out for a moment please." He stepped outside and went to her side, putting his hand around her shoulders.

"Thank you darling!" She said to him.

"We are going to try and sort this crazy mess out somehow."

"But how on earth could such stupid ideas enter these people's heads in the first place?" He asked.

"It's preposterous!"

"Bill dear, never mind. It's all a dreadful confusion which will be cleared up soon enough," she assured him.

The lightning flashes and occasional claps of thunder continued and the group began to show signs of restiveness. Ziboere held one of Bilflow's hands in hers and beckoned on the leader to come closer. He did not bulge. It was obvious that the people, for whatever reason, were somehow scarred of her.

"If you refuse to come close to us, we will come to you," she threatened. When he still would not move, they marched firmly towards him, halting about three feet from him. All watched curiously wondering what she was up to. She looked at Bilflow and smiled reassuringly at him, then turned and faced the crowd, staring unblinkingly at the leader and began to speak again. The speech was long and touched on many issues fundamental to human existence. At this, a hush again fell on the crowd.

"My dear brothers and sister," she began.

"Yes, we are all related even though you may not know it. Your leader has said that my husband used evil powers to cause untold calamities in your homes. You believe that if a sacrifice of a cock and some other things is made, your god will be appeased, thereby ending your misfortunes. Oh, you blind of the earth! Have you looked within yourselves and at your surroundings before rushing here to blame us? If you cannot understand different circumstances in life why not ask people who are knowledgeable in such things. If you eat and sleep in filth, how can you be healthy? There are many things in your environment that can cause you harm. The Creator has provided everything for our welfare on earth and we have been given the power of thought, to think about ourselves, neighbors, environment and our world, seen and unseen. If I make you think seriously about what led you to match to our house this night, you will be amazed at what you will discover. If I make you think seriously about why your people are dying every day, you will be surprised at what will be revealed from within yourselves. But thinking is hard work and we prefer others to do the hard work for us. It is always easier to apportion blame. You have beclouded your minds and your sense of objectivity because you are afraid to think." She surveyed the group more closely and went on.

"…Yet, you expect all the bounties of creation to be available to you. You envy others who are ready to work hard for a share of what life has to give. Yours lay waste, crying to be claimed but you spit on them in your ignorance. Come take me, your riches call out to you constantly but you shake them off always. They lie fallow and then die away and you cry endlessly for what you have missed."

Pausing with a set expression on her face and now commanding their full attention, she continued her 'lecture.' However, some did not find the lecture funny and were becoming quietly restive. The leader began to address her but she held up her hand, silencing him and continued.

"You show your emptiness and ineptitude by conveniently laying the blame on invisible witches and wizards for your predicament. You go about lamenting that but for this or that person whose spirit is tormenting you, you would have become the wealthiest merchant in town or the wisest person or the most respected! You carry on and on with frivolous claims so life steadily but surely passes you by. Ah, I see some of you shaking your heads in agreement or disagreement? I cannot tell. Am I beginning to reach you? Am I, perhaps, making you think just a little?"

The leader could no longer remain silent and he cut in roughly, forcing her to pause and listen to him.

"Madam…! Madam Forest..! You must stop all this kind of talk. You have abused and insulted us enough, you hear me!" The crowd was in support.

"Yes, it is enough!" They shouted.

"What kind of think are you telling us to think? If we don't think, how could we have come here this night ehn…? If we don't think how could we have consulted the oracle and taken the advice of the Orukareowei? We do think, you hear me! We are people who think, that is why we know that your husband used his magic to raise you from the dead, long after you had died. Yes, we think very, very well madam! We think-O..ooooo!"

He beat his chest heavily to drive home this point. I sighed.

What a pity! All this while, I had been outside close to where Zibo-ere and Bilflow stood. Now I turned to them.

"Zibo-ere, Bill, please let's go inside and leave these people alone. You are wasting your time talking to them. You can see that they are not interested in your words of wisdom."

Bilflow agreed with me, perhaps realizing the futility of the situation. He whispered something in Zibo-ere's ear.

"Why?" She asked.

"Because my darling, you do not change people who are bent on having their way. It will take, oh, heaven knows how long, may be forever, to change people in this mold," he told her in exasperation. She smiled at him.

"Sweetheart, be patient for just a while and give me a chance with them. Please, let me try and resolve this." Shaking his head in resignation, he reluctantly agreed.

"Okay darling, I'll stay until they leave. But remember my warning!"

He turned to me and shrugged his shoulders. Zibo-ere turned back to the group and asked the leader his name.

"Haaaa!" He exclaimed and looked at the others.

"She wants to know my name! Madam Oyibo, what do you want to do with my name ahnnn? If all those people could die just like that, when you or your husband did not know their names, why should I tell you my name? Do you take me for a fool, ehn? Do I look like a fool to you?" He asked rudely.

"Look madam, I can never, never tell you my name. Never!" He said with deliberate emphasis.

Then in a most bizarre act of self-contradiction, he turned to his group of comrades and beat his chest heavily.

"How can I, Odudu, knowingly walk to my death? Everyone knows I am a fearless man, a champion wrestler and a daring hunter. I am not afraid of natural death. Any time it comes, I am willing to stand and face it. Is that not so?" He asked.

"Yinn!" They answered enthusiastically, their apprehensions a short while ago all but forgotten. Zibo-ere, displaying inexhaustible patience called the leader once more.

"Odud!"

"Aah!" He answered automatically, before realizing that she had actually called him by name.

"You have known my name, madam. You tricked me into telling you my name. I hope you are satisfied now. Let me see what you will do with it now that you know it." He dared her in a deflated tone.

"My dear Odudu," she called and he flinched at the word 'dear.' But she continued.

"My dear Odudu, are you prepared to go home now with your people?"

"No way!" He hissed.

"The sacrifices must be made before we go, otherwise, the elders will not be satisfied. We cannot go home without you and your husband agreeing to our demands." He insisted, with the crowd supporting him. She tried to make them change their minds and leave but they were adamant and refused to move.

"Odudu, I appeal to you once more. Take your people and go home. Your problems are not going to be solved by animal sacrifices. Please go to your houses, it is almost morning now."

She cajoled, all to no avail. Then she seemed to make up her mind about something since they refused her plea. She sighed and told Odudu to get his cock and be ready for the sacrifice.

"Come out to this place," she said, pointing to a grassy area, "and prepare your sacrificial materials. But I sense that your cock is too small for such a big problem, am I correct?" She asked. He looked at her strangely.

"Yes madam. You are correct in that aspect." He agreed.

"Alright then, my brothers and sisters I am happy at that answer." She told them.

"Now that we have agreed on a bigger sacrificial material, let me produce it for you." Everyone waited in curious anticipation. She turned, took hold of her husband's hand and pushed him towards the leader.

"Odudu!" She called in a commanding tone.

"My husband will be your product of sacrifice. You said he has used his evil powers to cause suffering on your people and now he must pay. I agree with you that he must pay."

There was shocked silence as Odudu held Bilflow's hand. No less shocked of course, was Bilflow who stared at his wife, mouth agape. Still in the same tone of voice, she continued.

"Get your cutlass and some people to help you hold him down while you perform the sacrifice. I assure you, he will not struggle or object."

Three young men sprang to Odudu's assistance without invitation as he stood there undecided. The young men grabbed Bilflow and threw him to the ground as the crowd pushed forward to see what was happening. A cutlass materialized from somewhere and was shoved into Odudu's hand. The crowd urged him to invoke the spirits of their ancestors to witness the sacrifice. This was a normal practice and the people expected Odudu to follow the tradition to the full.

"Odudu, begin!" They urged.

"Start the incantations. Start chanting and call on the gods. What is the matter with you, Odudu? Start now!"

They pressed him but he just stood there and stared at them with a stupefied look on his face. After some time, one of the three volunteers spoke rudely to him and snatched the cutlass from him.

"I thought you said you were a fearless warrior." He sneered.

"Now that we have our prey in our hands, you are unable to perform. You want to shame us and stigmatize us as weaklings! I shall perform the sacrifice myself but you must pay the price for this disgrace. You Odudu, know that it is an abomination for a sacrificial animal not to be instantly killed upon being offered to the leader.

The gods will be very angry with you for behaving like a coward." He said, fuming. This young man turned to the people who were now enraged.

"My people, you know our custom. Odudu has shamed our ancestors and disgraced all of us here. Every one of us knows the penalty for this type of offence. So tell me my people, shall I apply our laws or do we leave him at the mercy of the gods?" Shouts of 'deal with him!' 'kill him!' Rented the air.

With the judgment passed on Odudu by his people, they let go of Bilflow and seized him. Odudu who was now visibly afraid, recovered his tongue and tried to find a way out of his dilemma.

"Look! Look here all of you." He began in a shaky voice. "I am your leader sent by the elders of our village. They chose me because I am fearless and …"

"Shut up, you coward!" Someone shouted at him. He tried again, this time with a shrill to his voice.

"Listen my people! Listen to me now! What madam Forest said is true, very true! I don't know what came over me just now when I was told to begin the sacrifice. Something seemed to seize me and I could not move…and…."

"Woo! Woo!" The crowd booed, not impressed with his explanation. The new self-appointed leader boasted that he could sacrifice Bilflow with one stroke of the cutlass. However, Odudu had to be dealt with first so that the gods could be temporally pacified and their anger not be carried over to any other person in the village. Odudu tried once more to talk them out of their line of reasoning, certain that their treatment of him was unjustified.

"Look my people, this is utter foolishness. From your behavior," he asserted, "I now believe that our treatment of Mr. Forest and his family was unjust." No one appeared moved or interested in his words.

"Let us stop and think please!" He was almost wailing now.

"There is no need to kill me as custom demands. I really do not deserve to die like this. Please, listen to me, my brothers and sisters. Don't kill me like this! I have not offended the gods! Please, let us stop and think very well for once!"

His plea was in vain. His comrades carried him out of the compound still shouting and raining abuses at him.

"Coward! Coward! Die like a man!" They shouted and trooped out with the doomed leader. As the last of them left, the maiguard gratefully closed the gate after them and locked it, shaking his head in bewilderment.

"What a day!" Bilflow sighed in relief. "Hmm! A day of love and a night of danger. What a day!"

"Let's all go to bed now and try to catch a few hours' sleep before dawn, if we can." Zibo-ere told everyone as we went into the house and locked the door.

Ebiere hugged her mother affectionately and scolded her in mock horror for putting her father's life in danger.

"That was a dangerous thing to do mama!"

"Trust me my angel, your father was never in danger out there." Zibo-ere told her, smiling.

GLOSSARY

Aaboo: Exclamation of surprise.
Man no be wood: Pidgin metaphor insinuating that a man needs the love of a woman.
Agene: A frenzied traditional dance.
Ama-Olotu: The Strongest man in the town as determined after a wrestling bout.
Anda-Olotu: Wrestling champion.
Atuu: Affectionate traditional mode of embrace.
Baiyo-o: Goodbye.
Banga Soup: Pidgin for soup prepared with palm fruit paste.
Diri: Medicine.
Diriguo-ere: A witch.
Diri-Olotu: A renowned traditional medicine practitioner.
Ebamua: You are not going back.
Efinkiriyo: Community square.
Fere: Earthenware food bowl.
IzonOttu: The entire Izon community nation, also anglicized as Ijaw.
Kokoma: Unique music of the fifties and early sixties.
Lufeyai: Soup prepared with palm fruit paste.
Maiguard: Gateman.
Nene: Mother.
OdogboroDein: A traditional marriage ceremony.
Ogele: Izon traditional dance.

Okodo: A traditional meal prepared with plantain/yams with fish/meat/shrimps/prawns.

Okoide-o: Respectful greeting of someone older than you by genuflecting.

Okoisine-o: Same as above for more than one person.

Okosu-ere: Old woman.

Oruama: Gods.

Orukare-ere: A high Priestess responsible for sacrifices at the shrine of the gods.

Orukari-owei: A high Priest responsible for sacrifices at the shrine of the gods.

Orutebo-owei: The leading high priest in the village.

Osun: A local delicacy prepared with processed cassava starch.

Owigiri: A contemporary Izon dance.

Oyibo: Colloquial or pidgin word for a Caucasians

Peletuwo: A mythical rejuvenation ritual or ceremony.

Penaowei: Izon word for a Caucasian.

Pulou-feyai: Palm oil soup prepared with or without unripe plantain/cocoyam/yam.

Remote Control Emi-o: There is black magic.

Seri-awoama: Response to the genuflection-get up children.

Sufferman: Pidgin for the downtrodden.

Temarau: Almighty Creator/God. She who created us-Izon world view.

Tamarau-e de bamo-o: You are great Almighty Creator.

Tufia: Traditional exclamation, rejecting something ominous or evil.

Waaka: Colloquial form of abuse, spreading all ten or five fingers at someone.

Woo! Woo!: Expression of displeasure by booing or expression of excitement.

Yinn: Affirmative response.

ABOUT THE BOOK

Love so pure is a driving force for animate beings who want to seek the hidden doors to the realities of creation. It serves as a preparatory recipe for one to meet his/her ultimate Creator through embracing the finest virtues of life such as tolerance, empathy, patience, peace and unconditional love.

To the sober seeker, the ideas contained herein are soothing tonic for the soul. The author has successfully animated the reader to embark on a spiritual voyage of self-discovery. It is a passionate recount of man's essence in life and the divine purpose of our creation in its complete and true form.

This book also captures a vivid theorization that the human soul lives again in a new body after someone's physical death.

ABOUT THE AUTHOR

Educated in the United States of America, Gesiere Brisibe-Dorgu holds a Bachelor of Arts degree in Political Science from the University of Minnesota, Twin Cities, Minnesota and a Master of arts degree in Public Administration from Mankato State University, Minnesota.

She is the founder and president of KEMSESE, Center for Young People in Need, a non-profit organization. Gesiere Brisibe-Dorgu is a self-taught visual artist.

www.ingramcontent.com/pod-product-compliance
Lightning Source LLC
Chambersburg PA
CBHW022012120526
44592CB00034B/795